DISCARD

STEVEN SPIELBERG

Director of Blockbuster Films

Laura B. Edge

Enslow Publishers, Inc.
40 Industrial Road
Box 398
Berkeley Heights, NJ 07922
USA

http://www.enslow.com

For Chris and Allison

Copyright © 2008 by Laura B. Edge

All rights reserved.

No part of this book may be reproduced by any means
without the written permission of the publisher.

Library of Congress Cataloging-in-Publication Data

Edge, Laura Bufano, 1953-
    Steven Spielberg : director of blockbuster films / Laura B. Edge.
        p. cm. — (People to know today)
    Summary: "A biography of film director Steven Spielberg"—Provided by publisher.
    Includes bibliographical references and index.
    ISBN-13: 978-0-7660-2888-3
    ISBN-10: 0-7660-2888-7
    1. Spielberg, Steven, 1946—Juvenile literature. 2. Motion picture producers and directors—
United States—Biography—Juvenile literature. I. Title.
    PN1998.3.S65E34 2008
    791.4302'33092—dc22
    [B]
                                                    2007017076

Printed in the United States of America

10 9 8 7 6 5 4 3 2 1

To Our Readers: We have done our best to make sure all Internet addresses in this book were active
and appropriate when we went to press. However, the author and publisher have no control over
and assume no liability for the material available on those Internet sites or on other Web sites they
may link to. Any comments or suggestions can be sent by e-mail to comments@enslow.com or to
the address on the back cover.

♻ Enslow Publishers, Inc., is committed to printing our books on recycled paper. The paper in
every book contains 10% to 30% post-consumer waste (PCW). The cover board on the outside of
each book contains 100% PCW. Our goal is to do our part to help young people and the
environment too!

Photos and Illustrations: Associated Press, pp. 37, 70, 87, 90, 93, 101; © Dreamworks / courtesy
Everett Collection, p. 97; Everett Collection, pp. 9, 15, 40, 50; Getty Images, pp. 1, 4, 7, 13; Photo
by Ilpo Musto / Rex USA / courtesy Everett Collection, p. 47; © Paramount / courtesy Everett
Collection, pp. 44, 67, 103; Time & Life Pictures / Getty Images, p. 81; © Universal Pictures /
courtesy Everett Collection, p. 76; Universal TV / Photofest, p. 29; © Warner Brothers / courtesy
Everett Collection, pp. 59, 63.

Cover Illustrations: Getty Images.

CONTENTS

Steven Spielberg

1
ONE MORE SCREAM

On July 1, 1974, Steven Spielberg stood on the deck of the *Orca* in the Atlantic Ocean off Martha's Vineyard in Massachusetts. He prepared to film a battle between three men and a shark. The scene was the climax of the movie *Jaws* and Spielberg was the director.

Jaws tells the story of a man-eating great white shark that terrorizes a New England beach community and the men who join forces to destroy the beast. Spielberg read the novel by Peter Benchley and longed to turn the story into a film. "I wanted to do *Jaws* for hostile reasons," he said. "I read it and felt that I had been attacked. It terrified me, and I wanted to strike back."[1] "Fear is a very real thing for me. One of the best ways to cope with it is to turn it around and put it out to others."[2]

Twenty-seven-year-old Spielberg had only directed

one feature film. *Jaws* was a huge production and filming was not going well. The production was behind schedule and over budget. Spielberg worried that if he did not do a good job directing *Jaws*, he would never get the chance to direct another film. He created special effects that had never been done before on the ocean, and he was petrified that they would not work.

The biggest problem was the shark. Great white sharks cannot be trained to act in movies. Spielberg and his special-effects team built mechanical sharks for *Jaws*. "We had a number of different shark components," he said, "the full shark, which I call The Great White Turd, a fin that was pulled through the water, a left-to-right shark, and a right-to-left-shark."[3] Spielberg named the sharks "Bruce," after his lawyer. Each of the twenty-five-foot monsters weighed about two thousand pounds and was made of welded tubular steel. They had flexible moving joints and were attached to a twelve-ton steel platform that sat on the ocean floor.

Construction of the shark took longer than expected, so Spielberg began filming scenes without it. He realized that the movie would be scary if he did not show the shark to the audience right away, if he merely suggested its presence. Spielberg filmed two-thirds of the movie without letting the audience see the great white. "I wanted the water to mean shark," he said.

A scene from 1975's *Jaws* shows the man-eating great white shark heading straight for marine biologist Hooper (Richard Dreyfuss) and shark fisherman Quint (Robert Shaw) aboard the *Orca*.

"The horizon to mean shark. I wanted the shark presence to be felt everywhere before I finally let people get a glimpse of the shark itself."[4] But eventually, in a movie about a shark, he needed to show the shark. He had run out of scenes to film on land. The shark *had* to work!

On the first attempt to film the shark, Bruce sank. On the second, his hydraulic system exploded. On the next attempt, the salt water ate away his plastic skin and exposed the mechanical devices inside. "Everything that could go wrong with the shark went wrong," said producer David Brown.[5]

While the production crew worked on Bruce, Spielberg faced a host of other problems. The set constantly drifted and Spielberg's complicated equipment had to be lined up again and again. Most of the cast and crew got seasick. It was sunny one day, cloudy the next, so the film they shot on the first day did not match the film they shot on the second. Storms rolled in and delayed filming.

Spielberg believed it was crucial that the audience never saw land or any other boats during the dramatic life-or-death struggle between the men and the shark. He wanted to stress the isolation the characters felt on the boat as they faced the killer fish. But it was summer on Martha's Vineyard, and filming was often delayed when smiling vacationers sailed into the shot and waved to the camera. There were so many problems the crew called the movie "Flaws." Spielberg wondered, "Was this film going to end my career, was I going to have to end my career on the water, which I didn't like anyway, and would I ever work again?"[6]

Then the *Orca* sank, along with two expensive cameras and a precious day's worth of film. Producers Richard Zanuck and David Brown thought long and hard about shutting down the project. "I was panicked," said Spielberg. "I was out of my mind with fear—not of being replaced, even though people were trying to fire me, but of letting everybody down."[7]

Spielberg plodded along in spite of all the delays and kept filming. Some days he got a few feet of useable film. Some days he did not get any. His original schedule ballooned from 55 days to 159 days. "Frustration was at fever-pitch," he said, "Brave men were reduced to tears and quiet men made big speeches to the sky. Man was not made to go out on the ocean twelve hours a day for five months!"[8] But he refused to give up. On September 15, 1974, a relieved Spielberg, along with Bruce and the cast and crew of *Jaws*,

Steven Spielberg with CBS Evening News anchorman Walter Cronkite on the set of *Jaws*.

A Real Shark Attack

While Spielberg and company struggled along in Martha's Vineyard, Ron and Valerie Taylor photographed great white sharks off the coast of Australia. Spielberg hired the husband and wife team of shark experts so he could mix real shark footage with shots of Bruce. During one session, the Taylors filmed a shark attacking a steel cage. The shark got caught in the cables connected to the cage, went berserk, and tore the cage apart. Spielberg used the spectacular footage in the film.

completed filming and headed back to Hollywood.

After months of editing, *Jaws* was ready for a sneak preview. It was shown on March 26, 1975, in Dallas, Texas. Spielberg closely watched the audience reaction. They laughed in all the right spots. They screamed in all the right spots—except one. "There's one more scream we can get from this movie," he told his producers.[9]

In the original version of the film, the shark attacked a character named Ben Gardner and separated his head from his body. When the severed head popped out of the hull of a submerged boat, the audience did not respond. The camera showed Matt Hooper's reaction before the severed head, so the audience was not surprised. Spielberg wanted to reshoot the scene so the head startled the audience.

Zanuck and Brown refused to pay to reshoot the scene. Spielberg spent three thousand dollars of his own money, built a boat like the one used in the film, and reshot the scene in his editor's swimming pool. The new version of the scene got one of the biggest screams in the film.

Jaws opened nationwide in June 1975. It quickly became the "must-see" movie of the summer and the most successful movie in the world up to that time. It was the first movie to earn more than 100 million dollars and the first summer blockbuster. "*Jaws* was a living nightmare that turned into a golden opportunity," said Spielberg. "The success of that picture gave me control of my films; gave me control of what movies I would be making for the rest of my life. And it sort of opened up just a treasure chest of opportunities for me."[10] *Jaws* secured Spielberg's place as a Hollywood director, a dream he had held since childhood.

2
CREATIVE NAUGHTINESS

Steven Allan Spielberg was born in Cincinnati, Ohio, on December 18, 1946. He was the much-loved first child of Arnold and Leah Spielberg. Steven's father was an electrical engineer. A technical genius, Arnold Spielberg helped design the first computers. Steven's mom was artistic and outgoing. She played classical piano and studied ballet. Steven enjoyed sitting on her lap as a toddler listening to her fill the house with the beautiful music of Bach and Beethoven.

The Spielbergs moved to Haddonfield, New Jersey, the year Steven turned three. They lived in a neat middle-class neighborhood with tree-lined streets and two-story Colonial-style houses. Steven became a big brother, first to his sister, Anne, and then to Susan and Nancy.

Steven had a reputation as a "wild creature" in New Jersey. He liked to tease and scare his younger sisters and the neighborhood children. He often hid outside his sister Anne's bedroom window at night and chanted, "I am the MOOOOOON!"[1] His sister screamed in terror. Arnold Spielberg worked long hours for his job and was rarely home. Steven's mom tolerated her son's behavior. "His badness was so original that there weren't even books to tell you what to do," she said.[2]

Steven Spielberg as a baby in the arms of his father, Arnold, and his mother, Leah, in 1947.

Steven's first pets were parakeets. His parents thought birds would be easy to care for because they lived in cages. Steven had other ideas. He took the parakeets out of their cages and trained them to live on the curtain rod. At one time, he had eight birds living on the rod. His room was a mess! "There would be birds flying around and birdseed all over the floor," said Steven's mother. "I'd just reach in to get the dirty clothes."[3]

Steven had many fears as a child—the clouds, the wind, the trees outside his window. He feared monsters under his bed and hiding behind a crack in his bedroom wall. He loved to watch television but was often frightened by what he saw. He cried for hours after he watched a program about snakes. After that, his parents did not allow him to watch much television. They also limited the number of movies he was allowed to attend. They did take eight-year-old Steven to the movie *Snow White and the Seven Dwarfs*. "When the wicked queen turned into a hag and a skeleton crumbled into pieces, I burst into tears and started shaking," said Steven. "For three or four nights I had to crawl into bed with my mom and dad."[4]

One way Steven handled his fear was to transfer it to his three younger sisters. "This removed the fear from my soul and transferred it right into theirs," he said.[5] Once, he told them an old World War II pilot was rotting in his closet. He put an aviator cap and

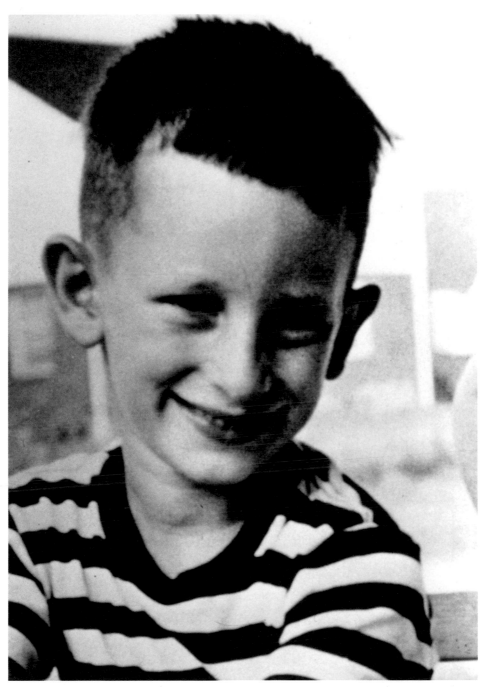

As a young child, Steven Spielberg devised creative ways to torment his sisters, evidence of an imaginative mind destined for moviemaking success.

goggles on a plastic skull with a light bulb inside. Then he dared his sisters to go into the closet. After his sisters were inside the closet, he switched on the light inside the skull and locked the door. "I used to do anything in my imagination to terrify them," he said. "I was terrible."[6]

The Spielbergs were Jewish, and Steven attended Hebrew classes three times a week. But he was ashamed of being Jewish. His family's religious beliefs made him feel different from his peers. "Being a Jew meant that I was not normal," he said. "I was not like everybody else. I just wanted to be accepted. Not for who I was. I wanted to be accepted for who everybody else was."[7]

The Christmas season was especially difficult for Steven. His neighbors decorated their homes with Christmas lights, plastic Santas, and scenes of baby Jesus in the manger. The Spielberg house stood out for its lack of decoration. Steven begged his parents to put up a few lights so their house would blend in with the others in the neighborhood. He was upset when his father refused.

In 1957, the Spielbergs moved to Phoenix, Arizona. The move was hard on ten-year-old Steven. "I was Jewish and wimpy," he said. "That was a major minority. In Arizona, too, where few are Jewish and not many are wimpy."[8] Steven did not enjoy school. He played the clarinet and studied just hard enough to pass to the next grade. His father tutored him in math, his least favorite subject. He was not very athletic and dreaded physical education class.

When Steven was twelve years old, Leah Spielberg bought her husband a movie camera for Father's Day. Steven thought his father's shaky home movies were boring. He thought he could make the movies more interesting, so Steven became the family photographer. He enjoyed being able to choose what to film. If a family scene lacked drama, he livened it up by staging the scene to add excitement.

> "I was **not** like **everybody** else."

Steven filmed the family camping trips. He forced his parents to stop the car before they reached the campsite so he could get out and film their arrival from just the right perspective. The family had to wait for Steven to yell "Action" before they could unload the car, set up the tents, or build a campfire.

Steven enjoyed staging train wrecks with his electric trains. His father grew frustrated with replacing the broken trains. Arnold Spielberg told his son that if he broke the trains one more time, he would take them away from him. Steven filmed *The Last Train Wreck* so that he could watch the demolition of his trains over and over again without the fear of losing them. He shot the trains crashing from different angles. He used little plastic men to add excitement to the scene. When Steven watched his film for the first time, he was "amazed at how my little trains looked like multi-ton locomotives."[9]

Steven's interest in filmmaking grew when he became a Boy Scout. He loved to tell stories around the campfire, especially ghost stories. He created a three-minute Western to earn a photography merit badge. "Not only did I get my merit badge," he said, "but I got whoops and screams and applause."[10] The positive reaction of his fellow Boy Scouts encouraged Steven to make bigger and better films. He made up his mind to become a professional film-maker.

> **". . . I got whoops and screams and applause."**

Steven's entire family helped out on his films. His father designed sets and worked on lighting and music. His sisters acted. His mom did anything and everything. She once boiled thirty cans of cherries jubilee in a pressure cooker until it exploded so Steven could film the gory mess. "He was always the center of attention," said Leah Spielberg. "Our living room was strewn with cables and floodlights—that's where Steven did his filming. We never said no. . . . Steven didn't understand that word."[11]

Steven often stayed home from school on Mondays so that he could edit the film he shot over the weekend. He placed a thermometer against a light bulb and held a heating pad over his face to make it look like he had a fever. When his mom came in to check on him, he moaned and groaned about how terrible he felt. Leah went along and let him skip school.

Filmmaking is an expensive hobby, and Steven needed to earn money to pay for film. He set up a home theater and charged twenty-five cents to show his films and rented films to the neighborhood children. His sisters sold soft drinks and popcorn. After each show, Steven quizzed the audience to see what they liked about each film and why. He used the popcorn and drink money to buy film for his next project. He donated the admission price to a local school for special needs children.

During World War II, Arnold Spielberg had been a radioman on a B-25 airplane and had fought the Japanese. He often told his son stories about the war, and Steven became fascinated with World War II. Steven began filming a fifteen-minute World War II movie, *Fighter Squad*, when he was in seventh grade. His father drove the cast to the local airport and Steven filmed his classmates in vintage fighter planes. He filmed in the cockpit and stood on the wings of the airplane to make it look like the plane was flying. He used ketchup for blood when the pilots were shot. He spliced documentary footage of World War II dogfights with the film he shot to create a realistic-looking film.

The cast and crew of the film thought making a

movie was an exciting game. But to Steven, it was serious. He wanted his movie to be perfect. "Here was this kid who was sort of a nerd and wasn't one of the cool guys," recalled Steve Suggs, one of the cast members. "He got out there and suddenly he was *in charge.* He became a totally different person."[12]

Steven started high school in September 1961. Small for his age, he was picked on by the other students, who called him "Spielbug." One school bully often knocked him down or held his head in the drinking fountain. "At school I felt like a real nerd, the skinny, acne-faced wimp who gets picked on by big football jocks all the way home from school," he recalled.[13]

In 1962, Steven filmed a forty-minute World War II movie called *Escape to Nowhere.* He convinced a bully who tormented him to act as the hero of the film. "I was able to bring him over to a place where I felt safer: in front of my camera," said Steven.[14] Steven filmed *Escape to Nowhere* in the desert around Camelback Mountain. His father helped him build battlefield props, and Steven created lots of realistic special effects for the battle scenes. *Escape to Nowhere* won first prize in a statewide amateur film contest.

Steven used the money and prizes he won for *Escape to Nowhere* on his next film. *Firelight* told the story of mysterious colored lights that appeared in the night sky and snatched people for an alien zoo.

Steven wrote the screenplay for *Firelight* and spent about six months filming in various locations around Phoenix. He called a local hospital and asked to borrow a room. He put one of his actresses in a bed and put an oxygen mask on her to shoot a scene. He bought his first sound system and recorded sound directly on the film.

Steven wrote the soundtrack for *Firelight* on his clarinet. His mother transposed the music and made sheet music. The high school band recorded it. Friends helped with advertising. They made signs and billboards and plastered them around Phoenix announcing that the film would be shown in a local theater.

On March 24, 1964, a seventeen-year-old Steven Spielberg stepped out of a limousine in front of the Phoenix Little Theater. A searchlight swept the night sky and flashbulbs exploded all around him. It was a special night for Steven—the premier of *Firelight,* his first feature-length film. The film cost

Out of this World

Steven got the idea for *Firelight* from an experience he shared with his father. When Steven was ten years old, his father woke him up in the middle of the night and rushed him outside and into the car. The pair drove to the outskirts of town, where Arnold Spielberg took out a blanket and spread it on the ground. Steven and his dad lay on the blanket and watched a fantastic meteor shower. "It was my first introduction to the world beyond the earth," said Steven. It filled him with the desire "to tell stories not of this world."[15]

less than six hundred dollars to make and ran for two hours and fifteen minutes. It was a rousing success. The packed theater made Steven his first profit as a filmmaker.

The next day, Steven and his family moved to northern California where Steven would face the biggest challenges of his life.

3
LEARNING THE BIZ AT UNIVERSAL STUDIOS

In March 1964, the Spielbergs move to Los Gatos, a suburb of San Jose, California, where Steven completed his junior year of high school. After the school year ended, the family moved to Saratoga, an affluent suburb in the foothills of the Santa Cruz Mountains. While his parents and three sisters spent the summer settling in Saratoga, Steven got the opportunity of a lifetime—the chance to hang out at Universal Studios in Los Angeles.

Steven maneuvered his way onto the Universal lot with the help of a man named Chuck Silvers. Silvers worked in Universal's editorial department and was in charge of reorganizing their film library. One of Arnold Spielberg's friends in the computer industry knew Silvers and asked him to give Steven a tour of the studio. Silvers agreed and was immediately impressed with Steven's enthusiasm and his vast knowledge of filmmaking.

Chuck Silvers hired Steven to work as an unpaid clerical assistant in Universal's editorial department. Steven ran errands, sorted paperwork, and helped out with odd jobs. He watched films and television shows being shot and talked with actors, editors, directors, and writers. "I visited every set I could, got to know people, observed techniques, and just generally absorbed the atmosphere," said Steven.[1]

Steven and Chuck Silvers often chatted about filmmaking, and Steven brought in several of his 8-mm films and showed them to Silvers. Steven's unmistakable talent greatly impressed Silvers. "Steven was such a delight," he said. "That energy! Not only that impressed me, but with Steven, nothing was impossible."[2]

When school started again in September, Steven had to tear himself away from Universal Studios and drag himself to a new school. His senior year was a difficult and painful time for him. "I encountered savage racial prejudice, even physical abuse," he said.[3] Classmates taunted him because he was Jewish and struck him in the hallways between classes. To mock the stereotype of Jews being greedy, some of his study hall classmates threw pennies at him. "I remember the sound of pennies landing all around my desk," said

Steven. "In that quiet study hall every penny sounded like the explosion of a bazooka."[4]

At home, Steven faced another kind of stress. His parents often quarreled and their marriage teetered on the brink of collapse. "I don't think they were aware of how acutely we were aware of their unhappiness—not violence, just a pervading unhappiness you could cut with a fork or a spoon at dinner every night," he said. "For years I thought the word 'divorce' was the ugliest in the English language."[5]

After graduation, Steven wanted to go to college to study filmmaking. But he had spent more time making films than he had studying, and his grades were mediocre. He could not get into California's top film schools, UCLA and USC. Instead, he enrolled in California State College at Long Beach. Cal State did not have a film department, so Steven studied English.

Arnold Spielberg moved to Los Angeles the summer Steven graduated from high school. Steven lived with his father in L.A. so that he would be close to the Cal State campus. Leah filed for divorced in April 1966. She and Steven's sisters moved back to Arizona.

During the 1960s, when Spielberg attended college, some young people on college campuses experimented with drugs and alcohol. Steven was not one of them. He saw his friends abuse drugs and did not want any part of that experience. "I never understood how they could ruin their lives with what I used to call a 'daylight sleep,'" he said. "I know that drugs are supposed to open you up, but what I saw was that they focused you down."[6]

Steven took classes at Cal State two days a week and spent the rest of his time at Universal Studios trying to get studio executives to watch his 8-mm films. "They were embarrassed when I asked them to remove their pictures from the wall so I could project my little silent movies," he said.[7] The studio bosses told Steven to make a 16-mm or 35-mm film and then they would watch it. The larger film size was expensive, so Steven worked in the college cafeteria to earn film money.

In 1967, Steven met George Lucas, a student at USC, at a student film festival. Lucas's futuristic film, *THX 1138:4EB*, was one of the films shown at the festival. Spielberg was awestruck by the film and by the realization that there were other passionate young filmmakers like him. He became even more determined to make a 16-mm or 35-mm film that he could show to Universal. This caused friction between Steven and his father because Arnold Spielberg felt Steven was not focusing enough on his college classes. Steven moved into a house in West Los Angeles with fellow student Ralph Burris.

The following year, Steven met Denis Hoffman, a young man who dreamed of becoming a movie producer. Steven told Hoffman about his plan to make a 35-mm film and Hoffman raised ten thousand dollars to finance it. Steven wrote the story. It told of a boy and girl who fall in love and then drift apart while hitchhiking from the Southern California desert to the Pacific Ocean. It was called *Amblin'*.

The twenty-six minute film took ten days to shoot. Steven filmed it in Palm Desert, California, in July 1968. Temperatures often rose above one hundred degrees. Spielberg spent six weeks editing the film. He worked from 4:00 P.M. to 4:00 A.M. each day, seven days a week, in a borrowed editing room. The film did not contain any dialog so Steven added a musical soundtrack.

When the film was completed, Steven called his friend Chuck Silvers and asked him to watch it. "When I saw *Amblin'*," said Silvers, "I cried. It was everything it should have been. It was perfect."[8] Silvers was so moved by the film that he called Sidney J. Sheinberg, the director of television operations for Universal Studios, and asked him to watch it.

> **"When I saw *Amblin'*, I cried."**
> —Chuck Silvers

Sheinberg watched *Amblin'* and thought it was terrific. The next morning he called Chuck Silvers and asked him to set up a meeting with Spielberg. At that meeting, Sheinberg offered Spielberg a job at Universal Studios. "You should be a director," Sheinberg told Spielberg. "I think so, too," said Spielberg.[9]

Sheinberg offered Spielberg a seven-year contract to direct television shows. Spielberg dropped out of college, signed the contract, and became the youngest filmmaker ever signed to a long-term Hollywood contract. Spielberg did not want to direct television shows. He wanted to direct movies. But he realized that directing television would be good training. He also hoped that once Universal Studios employed him, he would find a way to convince the decision makers to let him direct feature films.

Steven raced back to tell Chuck Silvers the news. He wanted to thank Silvers for helping him so he asked Silvers what he could do to repay his kindness. Silvers asked for two things. The first was a promise from Steven that when he made it big he would help young people struggling to break into the business. Silvers's second request was more personal. "Every time we meet I would like a hug," he said.[10] Spielberg has kept both promises.

Spielberg's first assignment at Universal was to direct an episode for a weekly television series called *Night Gallery*. Joan Crawford, an Academy Award winning actress, played the lead role. Spielberg feared that sixty-two-year-old Crawford would resent working with a twenty-two-year-old director. He also worried that the crew would not take him seriously because he looked very young for his age. The average age of the Hollywood workforce at that time was fifty-five.

His first experience as a professional director was far from blissful. Joan Crawford often forgot her lines. Then she became ill and filming was delayed until she recovered. The production fell behind schedule. Spielberg used unusual camera angles and shot in non-traditional ways. When the producer of *Night Gallery* viewed Spielberg's scenes, he did not like them. He reshot several scenes with a different director.

A young Steven Spielberg directs actress Joan Crawford on the set of the television program *Night Gallery* in 1969.

Spielberg was shocked that his work was not viewed as a complete success. He was crushed. "The pressure of that show was too much for me," he said. "I decided to take some time off, and Sid Sheinberg had the guts to give me a leave of absence."[11]

During his one-year leave of absence from Universal, Steven spent his time writing screenplays. After a while, he grew antsy and wanted to get back to work. "I suffocated in the freedom," he said. "I needed to work, and I came back to Universal and said, 'I'll do anything.'"[12]

Spielberg directed television programs for Universal from 1970 to 1971. In the process, he regained his confidence. "TV taught me to think on my feet," he said. "Either you roll with it or it rolls over you."[13]

Before long, he grew tired of directing TV episodes. He did not enjoy working with characters that were already established and in a format already determined by the series. He wanted to create his own vision, not work within the parameters of someone else's vision. He learned the skills of directing but had little freedom to experiment. He wanted to direct movies!

Spielberg got his chance in the fall of 1971 when he was hired to direct a television movie called *Duel.* It was a film that changed his life.

4

I WANT A HIT!

In *Duel,* a gigantic truck chases a traveling salesman as he drives to a meeting. For no apparent reason, the truck tries to run the salesman off the road. *Duel* was the first of many films to contain one of Spielberg's favorite themes—an ordinary person faced with an extraordinary situation who overcomes his fear and becomes a hero. *Duel* is a two-character drama, a man against a truck. Spielberg cast Dennis Weaver as the man. He took just as much care casting the truck.

Spielberg had very definite ideas about the appearance of the truck he wanted to use in *Duel.* Wally Worsley, the production manager, brought several trucks to the Universal back lot. Spielberg chose a rusty, mud-spattered gasoline tanker truck with a huge front end. He then added hydraulic tanks to both sides of the doors and covered the windshield with dead bugs. Finally, he gave the truck "a bubble bath of motor oil and chunky-black and crud-brown paint."[1] The effect was ominous and evil looking. "I wanted the truck to become the personified villain," he said.[2]

Spielberg sketched out a storyboard of the movie that showed what would happen in each scene. This helped him visualize and plan out the film. Then he had an artist paint the entire map on long sheets of paper. Spielberg wrapped the mural around the walls of his hotel room. He studied it each night so he would be prepared for shooting and stay on schedule. As he filmed the movie, he wrote notes on the mural and crossed off completed scenes. Spielberg filmed *Duel* on a lonely stretch of highway forty miles north of Los Angeles. He used as many as five cameras at once, set up at various locations, and shot the film in just sixteen days.

Spielberg had less than two weeks to edit *Duel*. He had to cut two and a half hours of film down to seventy-four minutes. He hired four editors, wore roller skates, and skated from one editing room to the next. *Duel* was shown on television on November 13, 1971. The response was overwhelmingly positive. It impressed studio executives, audiences, and critics. Novelist Stephen King expressed the thoughts of many when he wrote, "*Duel* is a gripping, almost painfully suspenseful rocket ride of a movie."[3]

Universal executives were so thrilled with the response to *Duel* that they asked Spielberg to add fifteen minutes to the film so it could be released as a feature film in Europe. In 1973, the expanded version was released in Europe, Australia, and Japan. It became a sensation.

After the success of *Duel,* Spielberg received dozens of offers to direct feature films. He chose *The Sugarland Express.* Based on a true story, *The Sugarland Express* tells the tale of Lou Jean and Clovis Poplin. The couple, desperate to retrieve their two-year-old son from a foster home, kidnaps a Texas highway patrolman, hijacks his squad car, and leads police on a frantic high-speed chase across Texas. Spielberg was drawn to the story because he identified with its theme—a child's separation from his parents. Spielberg knew the pain of separation. He had experienced it firsthand when his parents divorced.

Spielberg wrote the story and Hal Barwood and Matthew Robbins turned it into a screenplay. Producers Richard Zanuck and David Brown agreed to let Spielberg direct *Sugarland* if he could find a movie star to play the leading role. Spielberg was thrilled when Academy Award winning actress Goldie Hawn agreed to play Lou Jean.

To make the movie look authentic, Spielberg filmed the entire thing in Texas. He cast two Texas Rangers in the film and hired lots of locals from

Houston, Dallas, and San Antonio for the sixty-five other speaking roles. Filming began in January 1973. In the true story on which *Sugarland* is based, more than one hundred police cars were involved in the chase. Spielberg only had enough money in his budget for forty cars. He used a long lens to make the forty look like one hundred.

Just before the opening of *The Sugarland Express,* Spielberg panicked. He did not think audiences would like the film because it had a sad ending. "I want a hit!" he told his producers. "Let's change the ending. Let's make it a happy ending." Richard Zanuck and David Brown refused to reshoot the ending of the film. "In my moment of weakness, they put some backbone into me again," said Spielberg.[4]

The Sugarland Express did not do well at the box office, but the critics loved it. Pauline Kael of the *New Yorker* wrote, "This film is one of the most phenomenal directorial debut films in the history of movies."[5] Spielberg was not pleased. "I would have given away all those reviews for a bigger audience," he said.[6] He missed the cheers and applause he remembered from his fellow Boy Scouts. He wanted crowds of people to watch and enjoy his films.

In May 1973, Spielberg visited the office of his *Sugarland* producer Richard Zanuck. On his way out he spotted a pile of unpublished novels. The one on the top of the pile said *Jaws*. Intrigued, Spielberg swiped the manuscript and read it over the weekend.

On Monday morning, Spielberg burst into Zanuck's office and asked if he could direct *Jaws*. Spielberg loved the last part of the book, where the three men unite to fight the shark. He did not like the subplot that described a love triangle between the chief of police, his wife, and the shark expert. He thought it slowed down the story. Also, Spielberg did not think the characters in *Jaws* were likeable. He worried that the audience would root for the shark instead of the people.

Spielberg wanted to add humor to the story, cut out the love triangle, and focus the script on the excitement of hunting the killer shark. He insisted on massive changes when the book was converted into a screenplay. Several authors, including Peter Benchley, the author of the novel, spent months working on various versions of a script.

The script changed constantly during filming. Spielberg and Carl Gottlieb, who played the editor of the Amity newspaper in the film, spent hours each night working on the script for the next day. They often sat around the dinner table with the actors and discussed scenes. One of the major changes was the ending. In the novel, the shark ate Matt Hooper, the character played by Richard Dreyfuss. In Spielberg's version, Hooper survived. In changing the ending,

Spielberg gave the audience what they wanted to see. They cheered when the good guys won and the shark was blown to bits.

One of the benefits Spielberg reaped from the success of *Jaws* was that he became a very wealthy man. He bought a mansion in Coldwater Canyon near Beverly Hills and hired his production designer, Joe Alves, to decorate it. Spielberg filled his new home with all of his favorite toys—computer games, pinball machines, and a pool table. He covered the walls with framed movie posters and piled books, scripts, and movie soundtrack albums all around the house. Things were going well in his personal life, too. In 1976, Spielberg met actress Amy Irving and they began dating.

The success of *Jaws* also gave Spielberg something more precious to him than money—creative freedom. For years, ever since he made *Firelight* as a teenager, he wanted to make a film about UFOs. He had researched accounts of UFO sightings, read everything he could get his hands on, and interviewed scientists, pilots, and people who believed they had seen a UFO. He had written a screenplay and tried to get studio executives interested in making the film. No one was interested. Then, with the success of *Jaws*, everyone was interested. "I discovered what a hit can do for a filmmaker," he said.[7]

The film was *Close Encounters of the Third Kind.* The title refers to the three levels of evidence for

Spielberg with Amy Irving
in New York, 1984.

UFOs. A close encounter of the first kind
is sighting a UFO. The second kind is
physical evidence, like a part of a spacecraft. A close
encounter of the third kind is direct contact with an
alien.

Close Encounters was shot in early 1976 in Mobile,
Alabama; Devils Tower Mountain in Wyoming;
California; New Mexico; and Bombay, India. The
soundstage in Alabama was larger than two football fields and six times larger than any Hollywood

soundstage. Sometimes it took Spielberg more than eight hours to set up a thirty-second shot. "I'm not the easiest person to work with in terms of my crew," Spielberg admitted. "When I say I think something should take two hours, and they say four and then it takes six, I get angry. I lost my temper and walked off *Close Encounters* five times. I walked off and [then] cooled off."[8]

Spielberg worked hard to keep the plot of the film secret. He wanted to surprise the audience. He hired a team of security guards to make sure no one entered the set without the proper identification. Spielberg was even tossed off the set once when he forgot his ID badge. He did not allow anyone connected with the film to talk about it in interviews. When a reporter tried to find out the plot from Richard Dreyfuss, the star of the film, he said, "If I told you anything, Steven would kill me."[9]

In Close Encounters, Spielberg proved he worked well with child actors. In one scene, four-year-old Cary Guffey stood at his kitchen door and saw the aliens for the first time. Spielberg wanted the child's reaction to change from fear to amusement to joy. To accomplish this, the director set up two cardboard partitions. Behind the first partition stood Bob Westmoreland, the makeup man, dressed in a gorilla suit. Behind the second, stood Spielberg, dressed as the Easter bunny. With cameras rolling, a crew member removed the first partition. Cary saw the gorilla and looked startled and afraid. Then Spielberg appeared from behind the second partition and Cary smiled at him. Finally, Spielberg asked Westmoreland to take off his gorilla head. He did, and Cary laughed. The response was exactly what Spielberg wanted from the scene.

It took five months to shoot *Close Encounters* and another year to add the special effects. Studio executives were nervous about whether the film would make a profit. It had gone way over budget. Many people connected with the film industry speculated that Spielberg had peaked as a director and would never make another film as successful as *Jaws*.

In May 1977, Spielberg and his friend George Lucas flew to Hawaii for a vacation. Lucas was nervous about the release of his new film, *Star Wars*. Previews had not gone well, and Lucas feared he had made a disaster. Spielberg tried to take his friend's mind off his worry. For luck, the two directors built an elaborate sand castle on the beach. While they worked, Spielberg and Lucas talked about the movies they wanted to make.

Lucas told Spielberg his idea for a film about a treasure-seeking archaeologist. Spielberg loved the idea. He

Star Wars Takes a Bit Out of *Jaws*

George Lucas had no need to worry about the success of *Star Wars*. It quickly bumped *Jaws* out of first place as the biggest moneymaker of all time.

A scene from Steven Spielberg's *Close Encounters of the Third Kind*.

and Lucas shared a fondness for the old adventure serials of the 1930s and 1940s. They wanted to make a modern film in that style with lots of action and where good always triumphed over evil. By the time the sand castle was finished, Spielberg and Lucas had agreed to work together on *Raiders of the Lost Ark*, with Spielberg as director and Lucas as executive producer. They shook hands on the deal and agreed that if *Raiders* was a hit, they would make two sequels.

When *Close Encounters* opened in November 1977 it was a critical and commercial success. "What lifts this film into orbit—and what saves it from being a shaggy flying-saucer story," wrote movie critic Frank Rich, "is the breathless wonder that the director brings to every frame."[10] Spielberg was nominated for, but did not win, an Academy Award for Best Director for *Close Encounters*. But with two back-to-back hits, he was widely recognized as one of the hottest young talents in Hollywood.

5
BLOCKBUSTERS

In 1978, Spielberg produced the film *I Wanna Hold Your Hand*. It was the first of many films he produced but did not direct. Producing gave Spielberg the opportunity to help aspiring young filmmakers and make sure films he believed in made it to the big screen.

The next film Spielberg directed, *1941*, was a big, expensive comedy. The story takes place in December 1941, just after the Japanese attack on Pearl Harbor during World War II. It tells of a fictional attack on Los Angeles and the widespread panic that swept through the city.

When *1941* was released, it made a profit at the box office, but the film was considered a flop for Spielberg. Most people thought it was too busy, too loud, and simply not funny. One critic likened the film to "having your head inside a pinball machine for two hours."[1] Spielberg admitted his disappointment in the film and said, "I'll spend the rest of my life disowning this movie."[2]

The year 1979 marked a low point in Spielberg's personal life as well. He and his girlfriend, Amy Irving, became engaged but broke up three months later. Spielberg did not spend a lot of time moping about his problems. He and his pal George Lucas were hard at work on his next film, *Raiders of the Lost Ark.*

Raiders of the Lost Ark is a swashbuckling adventure story about an archeologist named Indiana Jones. Jones goes on a quest to find the Ark of the Covenant, a Biblical artifact. Hitler's Nazi soldiers are also searching for the Ark, and Indiana Jones must use daring, fast thinking, and a whole lot of luck to overcome his enemies. *Raiders* is filled with nonstop action. "I've always made the kinds of films that I, as an audience, would want to see," said Spielberg.[3] "I love to grip an audience and watch them lean forward in their seats or flinch at a wreck or at something frightening. I like involving the audience on a level of total participation."[4]

Spielberg worked with four illustrators and storyboarded

The Money Man and the Dreamer

The producer manages all of the business and financial aspects involved in making a film. The director is the chief artistic force behind the film. He blends together all of the ingredients that make up the film, including the script, the actors, and the music.

Raiders in more detail than he had his previous films. Filming began in June 1980 and took place in England, France, Tunisia, California, and Hawaii. Despite the diverse locations, Spielberg was determined to complete the film on time and under budget, something he had not done on any of his previous films.

Spielberg used forty-eight tarantulas in the opening scene of *Raiders*. They were supposed to crawl all over Harrison Ford and Alfred Molina. But when filming began, Spielberg thought the hairy spiders looked too sluggish. "Why aren't they moving?" he asked. "They look fake."[5] The spider wrangler explained that all of the spiders were

Spielberg works on a miniature set for 1981's *Raiders of the Lost Ark*.

male and therefore quite docile. Spielberg told the wrangler to bring in some female spiders to liven up the males. When he did, the spiders took off running over Ford and Molina and also toward the crew! Filming stopped while many of them ran for their lives.

When Spielberg filmed the scene that trapped Indiana Jones and Marion Ravenwood in a pit full of snakes, he used cobras, pythons, boa constrictors, grass, and garter snakes. Spielberg wanted the set to look covered in snakes. "We have to get more snakes," he said when he saw the snakes the crew had so carefully arranged for filming. "We need about 7,000 snakes in addition to the 2,000 we have here to make it work."[6] Bushels of snakes were flown in from Denmark. Since there were ten cobras in the scene, Spielberg also flew in anti-venom serum from India and had a doctor and an ambulance standing by.

Karen Allen, who played Marion, was skittish about working with all those snakes. "Karen was so terrified of the snakes," said Spielberg, "she couldn't scream, and of course she had to. But all that came out was air." To solve this perplexing problem, Spielberg dropped a snake on her from above. "It landed on her like a pearl necklace, and she screamed on cue for a week," said Spielberg.[7]

While filming in Tunisia, the temperature hovered around one hundred thirty degrees. Several members of the cast and crew, including Harrison Ford, the star, suffered from severe stomachaches because they were not used to the local food. Ford was miserable. Spielberg had planned an elaborate fight scene between Ford's character, Indiana Jones, and a sword-wielding Arab. When Ford hobbled onto the set, Spielberg changed the scene. Instead of filming the complicated battle, which would have taken two days, Spielberg told Ford to pull out his pistol and shoot the swordsman. It took one hour to film the scene, and a grateful Harrison Ford left early and went to bed. The scene became an audience favorite.

While filming *Raiders* in exotic locations, Spielberg grew lonely. His new girlfriend, Kathleen Carey, was far away in California, and Spielberg felt he had nobody to talk to. He began to think about putting those feelings into a story about a lonely ten-year-old boy who longs for a friend. As the story developed in his mind, Spielberg decided the friend should be a creature from outer space. Spielberg discussed his ideas with screenwriter Melissa Mathison, who was on the set visiting her boyfriend, Harrison Ford. She agreed to write the screenplay for *E.T.: The Extra-Terrestrial.*

Spielberg credits George Lucas, his producer, with helping him stay on schedule filming *Raiders of the Lost Ark*. "On *Raiders* I learned to like instead of love," he said. "If I liked a scene after I shot it, I printed it. I didn't shoot it again seventeen times until I got one

I loved."[8] As a result, he finished ahead of schedule and under budget.

Steven Spielberg and George Lucas, 1985.

Raiders of the Lost Ark opened in June 1981. It quickly became the box office hit of the summer and put Spielberg back on top as a director. Spielberg received an Academy Award nomination for Raiders, but once again, he did not win.

After *Raiders*, Melissa Mathison worked closely with Spielberg to develop the story for *E.T.* "My inspiration for *E.T.* was my interest in outer space and UFOs and the divorce of my mom and dad, which is, I think, what *E.T.* essentially is about," said Spielberg.[9] The director had another reason for wanting to make *E.T.* "I've always wanted to do something about kids because *I'm* still a kid," he said.[10]

E.T.: The Extra-Terrestrial tells the story of Elliott, a ten-year-old boy, who befriends an alien that was accidentally left behind on earth. Spielberg considers *E.T.* his most personal film. Elliot and E.T. express the same feelings of loneliness and longing for friendship that Spielberg felt as a child. "There's a lot of my life in the film," he said. "All the kids are combinations of my family and me."[11]

On *E.T.* Spielberg acted as both producer and director. Filming began in September 1981. He did not create storyboards for the film. "I decided, this once, to take a chance. Just came on to the set and winged it every day and made the movie as close to my own sensibilities and instincts as I possibly could."[12]

Spielberg often explained a scene and then asked the children what they would say if the situation really happened to them. When Elliot shows E.T. his toys, Henry Thomas, the actor who played Elliot, made up the dialog on the spot as if he were really showing his toys to a new friend.

Spielberg and the children in *E.T.* became very close. Spielberg and Henry Thomas spent every lunch hour playing video games together. Henry thought of Spielberg as his teacher. For Halloween, Spielberg surprised Henry by arriving at the set dressed as a teacher—an old lady teacher—complete with high heels, jewelry, and a hat. He worked the entire day dressed as the old lady.

Carlo Rambaldi, a sculptor, created the character E.T. at a cost of 1.5 million dollars. Spielberg wanted the creature to have eyes like the poet Carl Sandburg or the scientist Albert Einstein and a bottom like Donald Duck's when he waddles. "I wanted a creature that only a mother could love," said Spielberg.[13] During filming, the children forgot that E.T. was not real. Everyone on the set treated him as if he were a real person.

E.T.: The Extra-Terrestrial opened in June 1982. It broke all box office records, knocked *Star Wars* out of first place as the biggest moneymaker of all time, and received glowing reviews. "*E.T.* is a miracle movie," wrote Richard Corliss in *Time* magazine, "and one that confirms Spielberg as a master storyteller of his medium."[14]

E.T. was nominated for nine Academy Awards, including Best Director and Best Picture. It won four awards, including one for John Williams's music. Spielberg did not win as director nor as producer.

Spielberg showed *E.T.* to President and Nancy Reagan

E.T.'s Favorite Candy

The script called for Elliot to use M & M's to lure E.T. out of hiding. Mars Candy executives refused to grant permission to use their product in the film because they thought E.T. looked scary and might frighten children. The Spielberg team then approached Hershey Chocolate and asked permission to use Reese's Pieces. They agreed, and Reese's sales increased by sixty-five percent after the film came out.

Spielberg with the extraterrestrial star of 1982's *E.T.*

at the White House and to Queen Elizabeth II in England. He also showed the film to the staff of the United Nations, where he was awarded the U.N. Peace Medal. "The film has always been a celebration of friendship and love and promoting understanding between races and cultures," he said.[15]

In the summer of 1982, Spielberg released another film, a horror movie about ghosts invading a suburban home. The movie was called *Poltergeist*, which means "noisy ghost." "I love ghost stories. I've always loved them," he said. "I used to frighten my sisters with them. I used to frighten myself with them. I just like telling ghost stories."[16]

Spielberg wrote and produced *Poltergeist*. Tobe Hooper directed it. Spielberg storyboarded most of the movie and was on the set for the majority of filming. With *Poltergeist* and *E.T.* in theaters at the same time, Spielberg had two hits at once. "*Poltergeist* is what I fear and *E.T.* is what I love," he said. "One is about suburban evil and the other is about suburban good."[17]

> **"I love ghost stories. I've always loved them."**

In the midst of Spielberg's record-breaking summer success, a real-life tragedy occurred on the set of *The Twilight Zone*, a movie Spielberg produced. During filming, a helicopter crashed into three of the film's actors. Vic Morrow and two small children were killed in the accident. The director of the film, John Landis, stood trial for involuntary manslaughter. After a lengthy trial, he was found not guilty. Spielberg was investigated too, but since he was not on the set the night of the accident, he was cleared of any wrongdoing.

"This has been the most interesting year of my film career," said Spielberg. "It has mixed the best, the success of *E.T.*, with the worst, the *Twilight Zone* tragedy. A mixture of ecstasy and grief. It made me grow up a little more."[18]

6

A Film Company and a Movie For Grown-ups

Steven Spielberg wanted his own film production company. "I dream for a living," he said. "Once a month the sky falls on my head, I come to, and I see another movie I want to make. Sometimes I think I've got ball bearings for brains; these ideas are slipping and sliding across each other all the time. My problem is that my imagination won't turn off."[1] With his own production company, Spielberg could bring more of the films in his head to the big screen.

In 1982, he formed Amblin Entertainment. The company was named after the film that resulted in his first contract with Universal Studios. Universal built a southwestern-style studio complex on a secluded corner of their lot for Amblin.

Spielberg designed the complex, right down to the baked adobe bricks. "We need to work in a creative environment in order to stimulate our own natural creativity," he said.[2] Amblin had editing rooms, conference rooms, a day-care center, and a theater with a popcorn maker and candy counter. It also had a full-scale gym, a video game room, and a huge kitchen with a chef. Navajo pottery, woven rugs and baskets, and lots of plants filled the rooms. Fruit, olive, and palm trees dotted the landscape and near the front entrance was a wishing well with a miniature Bruce, the shark from *Jaws*. Universal spent 3.5 million dollars on Spielberg's studio. Spielberg called it his "home away from home."[3]

Amblin Entertainment produced a number of films in the 1980s, including *Gremlins*, *The Goonies*, *Back to the Future*, and *Young Sherlock Holmes*. Some of the films, like *Back to the Future*, were box office successes. Others were not.

In addition to his new office, Spielberg owned a mansion in Los Angeles, a beach house in Malibu, a four-acre estate in East Hampton on Long Island, and an apartment in the glitzy Trump Tower in New York City. In spite of all his

Only Two Stories

At Amblin Entertainment, the buildings are no higher than two stories because Spielberg is afraid to ride in elevators. He has often said that he will not go into an elevator alone because he knows the thing will get stuck between floors and his whitened bones will be found two weeks later.

wealth, his friend, director Bob Zemeckis, considers Spielberg a "regular" guy. "Sure he drives a Porsche, but he'll still pull into a 7-11 and buy a Slurpie," said Zemeckis.[4]

The next film Spielberg directed, *Indiana Jones and the Temple of Doom*, was the second of three Indiana Jones films he promised to make with George Lucas. When he traveled to India to scout locations for *Temple of Doom*, Amy Irving, his former girlfriend, surprised him at the airport. Irving was in India working on a movie. The couple started dating again.

George Lucas and Steven Spielberg worked together on *Temple of Doom*. Lucas created the basic story. Spielberg included several scenes that had originally been planned for *Raiders of the Lost Ark* but had been cut from that film. When they needed to create a dinner scene, Spielberg wanted the menu to include the most horrible things they could think of. So, Spielberg, Lucas, and screenwriters Willard Huyck and Gloria Katz sat around and thought up the most disgusting things a person could eat—squirming baby eels, baked beetles, eyeball soup, and chilled monkey brains. They needed a scary scene and did not want to repeat themselves with snakes, so Spielberg asked Lucas, "What's worse than snakes?"[5] They decided on bugs—twenty thousand creepy, crawly bugs.

Spielberg created more than four thousand storyboards for the film and planned each scene in great detail. He had the production designer, Elliot Scott, build elaborate miniatures of various sets. Spielberg photographed the cardboard sets from different angles and studied the printed photographs. This helped him decide on the best way to shoot the many action scenes in the film.

Spielberg began filming *Indiana Jones and the Temple of Doom* in the spring of 1983. He filmed the outdoor scenes in Sri Lanka, a tiny teardrop-shaped island in the Indian Ocean. He worked the cast and crew twelve hours a day in jungle temperatures of one hundred thirty degrees.

In the opening scene, Willie Scott, played by actress Kate Capshaw, wears a very expensive, red sequined dress. The dress was one of a kind, made with authentic 1920s and 1930s beads and sequins. While filming a jungle scene, the dress was draped over a tree branch. An elephant ate the back out of the dress! Spielberg's schedule called for the opening scene to be filmed last. He had to fly the seamstress who made the dress from New York to London to repair it before he could film the opening scene.

The cast and crew flew to London to film the indoor scenes. Spielberg had the production designer build a roller-coaster ride on the soundstage for a mineshaft chase scene. While the actors safely whizzed around on the roller coaster at ten miles an hour, Spielberg filmed them at different speeds and from a variety of angles. The effects made it look like they were traveling much faster.

Indiana Jones and the Temple of Doom was released in May 1984. It earned millions for Spielberg and Lucas, but the critics did not like it. The violence in *Temple of Doom* generated a storm of controversy. Parents were offended and criticized Spielberg for making a movie that many considered unsuitable for children. Spielberg said publicly that "he would put his hand over a 10-year-old child's eyes rather than let the child see a key 20-minute segment" of *Temple of Doom.*[6]

Film critic Ralph Novak chided Spielberg and his producer George Lucas in *People* magazine. "If they had set out to prove that they could get away with anything—insult the intelligence of viewers and literally make them sick—they couldn't have done it more effectively," he wrote. "There are no heroes connected with this film, only two villains; their names are Spielberg and Lucas."[7]

As a result of the public outcry over *Temple of Doom* and other violent films, the Motion Picture Association of America revised the motion picture rating code. A new rating was added between the PG and R ratings, PG-13.

Spielberg was also criticized for making yet another adventure film. Many people considered his movies shallow and immature. Critics wondered if he would ever "grow up" and direct a serious film for adults. Spielberg wanted to silence their complaints. He had the huge audiences he craved. Now he yearned for respect and admiration from the film community. With his next film, *The Color Purple*, he hoped for full theaters *and* accolades from his critics.

The Color Purple is based on a Pulitzer Prize winning novel by Alice Walker. "When I read it I loved it," said Spielberg. "I cried and cried at the end."[8] It is the story of Celie, a poor African-American woman growing up in the south in the early 1900s. Although Spielberg loved the book, he worried that he might not be the right director for the movie. "Don't you want to find a black director, or a woman?" he asked producer Quincy Jones. Jones made it clear he wanted Spielberg to direct the film. "You didn't have to come from Mars to do *E.T.*, did you?" he said.[9]

Spielberg finally agreed. "I've got to do this for me," he said. "I want to make something that might not be everybody's favorite but, this year at least, is my favorite."[10]

Filming began in June 1985. On June 13, as Spielberg filmed a scene where Celie gives birth, Amy Irving went into labor with Spielberg's son Max. Spielberg finished filming the scene with Celie and then

Baby Talk

When Spielberg needed the sound of a baby crying for *The Color Purple*, he recorded Max crying at home and used it in the film.

rushed to the hospital to watch Amy deliver Max. Spielberg was thrilled to be a father and described Max as "my best production ever."[11]

Spielberg believes the ability to communicate is a key ingredient in a successful director. "Directing is eighty per cent communicating and twenty per cent know-how," he said. "If you can communicate to the people who know how to edit, know how to light, and know how to act—if you can communicate what you want so that what they're doing is giving you your vision, that's my definition of a good director."[12]

Spielberg often communicates by refer-encing movies. According to Whoopi Goldberg, who played Celie in *The Color*

Steven Spielberg directs Whoopi Goldberg on the set of 1985's *The Color Purple.*

Purple, "He'd say, 'The feeling of this scene is like how Jem felt when he first saw Boo Radley in *To Kill a Mockingbird.*'"[13] Since they both spoke the language of movies, Goldberg understood Spielberg's vision and delivered a heart-wrenching performance as Celie.

Steven Spielberg and Amy Irving were married on November 27, 1985, at the courthouse in Santa Fe, New Mexico. "I'm intolerably happy!" said Spielberg. "I've been dedicated to films before. Now, for the first time in my life, I'm committed to another person."[14]

The Color Purple was released in December 1985. It did well at the box office, and most critics gave it a positive review. Gene Siskel wrote in the *Chicago Tribune,* "*The Color Purple* couldn't have a sweeter, more uplifting tone. The director who tugged at our hearts with the rubber alien E.T. works at an even deeper emotional level with flesh-and-blood characters this time."[15]

Other critics were viciously negative and attacked Spielberg as well as the film. Gerald Early wrote, "*The Color Purple* is a very bad film, so undeniably bad that one wonders how Steven Spielberg—its director—ever acquired any sort of reputation as a competent artist."[16]

The Directors Guild of America gave Spielberg the Best Director award for *The Color Purple.* The film was also nominated for eleven Academy Awards. Although the film was nominated for Best Picture, Spielberg was not nominated for Best Director. It was the first time in history a Directors Guild winner failed to be nominated for an Academy Award. *The Color Purple* did not win a single Academy Award.

In 1985, Spielberg created a television series for NBC called *Amazing Stories.* He wrote fifteen of the first season's twenty-two stories and directed four episodes. *Amazing Stories* gave Spielberg a place to showcase some of his smaller ideas, stories that were not long enough to turn into feature films. It also gave him the chance to hire young film school graduates as first-time directors. *Amazing Stories* was shown on television from 1985 to 1987. It was an expensive show and did not do well in the ratings.

By the late 1980s, many Hollywood insiders considered Steven Spielberg the most powerful man in Hollywood. This gave him the freedom to take risks and make films that were important to him, regardless of their box office potential. He could ignore his critics and focus on telling the stories he wanted to tell.

7

FAMILY MAN

Spielberg's next project, *Empire of the Sun*, was what he called a transitional film. Like *The Color Purple*, it was a film that dealt with adult themes instead of childhood themes. He made the film just after he turned forty. "It's time to stop balls from rolling, and spaceships from landing, and the light shows," he said. "It's time to deal with what people say to each other when they have an emotional need to communicate."[1]

Empire of the Sun was adapted from J. G. Ballard's autobiographical novel. It is the story of Jim, a wealthy British schoolboy living in Shanghai, China, at the start of World War II. Jim is separated from his parents and thrown into a Japanese prison camp. He faces hunger, disease, and the horrors of war as he struggles to survive. "I wanted to draw a parallel story between the death of this boy's innocence and the death of the innocence of the entire world," said Spielberg.[2]

Spielberg wanted to shoot part of the film in Shanghai so that it would look authentic, but he needed permission from the Chinese government. After a year of negotiations, he obtained permission to shoot in Shanghai for twenty-one days. Since rickshaws were no longer used for transportation, Spielberg's crew built fifty to use in the film. They also replaced more than one thousand modern signs and billboards with signs with traditional Mandarin lettering.

Filming began in March 1987. Spielberg flew authentic 1930s cars,

Steven Spielberg (center) with the stars of his 1987 film, *Empire of the Sun*, Christian Bale (left) and John Malkovich (right).

Japanese tanks, and camera equipment to Shanghai. He hired ten thousand locals to appear in the film. After they completed the Shanghai scenes, the cast and crew traveled to England and Spain to film the rest of the movie.

Spielberg found it difficult to film scenes of a child in a prisoner of war camp. He suffered along with the character. "I'm always trying to infuse humor into any situation," he said. "The more dramatic the situation, the more fun I have trying to find the lighter side to the darkness. And in this case, I had to really bite my lip to drown out where my kick reflex from all my other films was taking me. It was a real internal struggle to get this thing on the screen and not mess it up."[3]

On March 31, 1987, Steven Spielberg was awarded the Irving G. Thalberg Memorial award at the Academy Awards ceremony. The award is given to "creative producers whose bodies of work reflect a consistently high quality of motion picture production."[4]

Empire of the Sun was released in December 1987.

Storytellers

In his acceptance speech for the Thalberg Award, Spielberg paid tribute to writers and said that filmmakers "are first and foremost storytellers." He talked about the importance of reading in order to inspire a new generation of writers. "In our romance with technology and our excitement at exploring all the possibilities of film and video, I think we've partially lost something that we now have to reclaim," he said. "I think it's time to renew our romance with the word."[5]

It received mixed reviews and earned only 66.7 million dollars worldwide. Spielberg considered it a box office failure, but he was proud of the film. "I knew I had to make this movie despite my producer hat, which kept nagging at me that this was not a movie to spend a lot of money on because you're not going to make any of it back," he said. "And yet some things need to be done regardless of the commercial return."[6] Although it did not receive any Academy Awards, *Empire of the Sun* was named Best Film of 1987 by the National Board of Review and was listed as one of the top ten films of the year by nearly seventy critics.

Spielberg turned from the box office disappointment of *Empire of the Sun* to what he knew would be a sure-fire hit, the third *Indiana Jones* film. Spielberg gave three reasons for making the film. He had promised his friend George Lucas he would make three films and he wanted to keep that promise. He also wanted to apologize to his fans for *Temple of Doom*, which he thought was too dark and horrific. "But the real reason I'm doing *Indy III* is because I want to have fun," he said.[7]

Lucas and Spielberg worked together to create the story for *Indiana Jones and the Last Crusade*. Lucas wanted the story to be about a quest for the Holy Grail, the chalice that once contained the blood of Jesus Christ. Spielberg wanted to make it a father-son story. "I wanted to do Indy in pursuit of his father, sharing his father's dream," said Spielberg, "and in the course of searching for their dreams, they rediscover each other."[8] Producer Lucas and director Spielberg compromised and created a story that combined the two ideas.

Filming began in May 1988. The movie was shot on four continents, in nine countries, and eight states. Spielberg enjoyed working with Harrison Ford as Indiana Jones and Sean Connery as his father. In many of the scenes between Ford and Connery, the actors improvised the dialogue during filming. "The biggest thrill was putting Harrison and Sean in a two-shot and calling 'Action!' and trying not to ruin the take by laughing," said Spielberg.[9]

In any *Indiana Jones* movie, there has to be some kind of scary, crawly creature. In the first film it was snakes. In the second, bugs. Ten thousand rats were the creepy stars of *Last Crusade*. "Rats was the follow up to the bugs which was the follow up to the snakes," said Spielberg.[10] In order to make sure the rats they used were not infected with a virus or disease that could harm the actors, rat breeders were hired to breed disease-free rats. For the scene in which the rats were killed, Spielberg's crew built one thousand mechanical rats so the live rats would not be hurt.

Indiana Jones and the Last Crusade was released in May 1989. It was Spielberg's biggest hit since *E.T.* and most critics considered it the best of the three *Indiana*

Jones films. Vincent Canby of the *New York Times* also noted that Spielberg demonstrated a new maturity in his direction of the film. "With *Empire of the Sun* and *Indiana Jones and the Last Crusade*, it is clear that his movies are growing up," he wrote.[11]

Sean Connery (in sidecar) and Harrison Ford in *Indiana Jones and the Last Crusade* (1989).

Spielberg's joy over the success of *Last Crusade* was clouded by sadness in his personal life. In May 1989, he and his wife, Amy Irving, announced they would divorce. The demands of two separate careers had taken its toll. They shared custody of their son Max, and Irving received a large financial settlement. The breakup was devastating for Spielberg.

To ease the pain of his personal life, Spielberg threw himself into work. In 1989, he directed a romantic fantasy called *Always*. He enjoyed working with the film's actors, Richard Dreyfuss, Holly Hunter, and John Goodman. When filming was completed, he gave each of them a brand new Mazda Miata with personalized license plates reflecting the characters they played. *Always* was released in December 1989. It received mixed reviews and did not do well at the box office.

Spielberg also produced several successful animated features, such as *An American Tail, The Land Before Time*, and *Fievel Goes West*. In 1990, he helped create cartoon characters and was the executive producer for the animated television series *Tiny Toon Adventures*.

About this time, Spielberg began dating Kate Capshaw, the actress who played Willie Scott in *Indiana Jones and the Temple of Doom*. "I fell wildly in love with his sweet face and his sweet heart," said Capshaw.[12] Capshaw was raised Methodist, but she converted to Judaism when her relationship with Spielberg grew serious. "I did it because I identified with the religion's emphasis on family," she said, "and I believed

A Jewish Mouse

An American Tail tells the story of a Jewish mouse who immigrates to America to escape the cats that persecute him in Russia. Spielberg named the main character, Fievel Mousekewitz, after his maternal grandfather, a Russian immigrant whose Yiddish name was Fievel.

Steven and I should be partners in our traditions and our faith."[13]

Steven Spielberg and Kate Capshaw were married on October 12, 1991, in a traditional Jewish ceremony at Spielberg's East Hampton estate. "I found true love with Kate," said Spielberg, "and I don't say that with a Harlequin romance feeling. I say it from the most honest part of me."[14]

They both wanted a large family, so Capshaw put her acting career on hold to care for their

> **"I have always felt like Peter Pan. . . . It has been very hard for me to grow up."**

growing brood. She had a daughter, Jessica, from a previous marriage and Steven had Max from his marriage to Amy Irving. They adopted Capshaw's African-American foster child, Theo, and had a daughter, Sasha, and a son, Sawyer, together.

Spielberg has often been called Hollywood's Peter Pan, the boy who refused to grow up. "I have always felt like Peter Pan," he said. "I still feel like Peter Pan. It has been very hard for me to grow up."[15] It came as no surprise, then, when he decided to direct a film about Peter Pan called *Hook*.

Hook is a modern day story of a grown-up Peter Pan who goes by the name Peter Banning. Banning, a man with no imagination and no sense of humor, must return to Neverland to rescue his children from

Spielberg and his wife, Kate Capshaw, arrive at the Kennedy Center for the Performing Arts in Washington. In 2006, he was honored for his contribution to American culture.

Captain Hook. In order to do this, he must recapture his childlike sense of wonder and relearn the skills he had as a child but no longer possesses as an unhappy adult.

Hook began filming in February 1991. It was the first Spielberg movie to be shot entirely on movie sound stages. The various sets filled nine stages, including Stage 27, where the 1939 classic *The Wizard of Oz* was filmed. Production designer Norman Garwood estimated that he used twenty-five thousand gallons of paint, two hundred sixty tons of plaster, ten miles of rope, and more than 1 million board feet of lumber building the sets. The budget ballooned to over 70 million dollars and *Hook* became one of the most expensive films ever made.

> **"I'm part of a generation that is extremely motivated by career."**

Hook was a very personal film for Spielberg. "I'm part of a generation that is extremely motivated by career," he said, "and I've caught myself in the unenviable position of being Peter Banning from time to time. I've seen myself overworked, and not spending enough time at home and I got a couple of good lessons from making the movie."[16]

Hook was released in December 1991. It did well at the box office but did not approach the profits of

Spielberg's blockbuster films. Most film critics did not care for *Hook*.

As Steven Spielberg headed into the 1990s he resolved to challenge himself as a filmmaker and create films with mature themes. "I'm trying to grow up in increments," he said. "I'm trying very gently to step up to a different kind of movie."[17] With his next two films, one a box-office bonanza and the other a cinematic masterpiece, Spielberg proved he was up to the challenge.

8
DINOSAURS AND
DEATH CAMPS

In the spring of 1990, best-selling author Michael Crichton mentioned to Steven Spielberg that he was working on a novel about dinosaurs and DNA. Spielberg told the writer that he had always been fascinated by dinosaurs and would love to read the novel. Crichton slipped Spielberg a copy of the unpublished manuscript, *Jurassic Park*. After he read the book, Spielberg called Crichton and told him he was interested in turning the book into a movie. "I'll give it to you if you guarantee me that you'll direct the picture," said Crichton.[1] Spielberg agreed. "With 'Jurassic' I was really just trying to make a good sequel to 'Jaws.' On land," he said.[2]

Spielberg worked on pre-production for *Jurassic Park* for two years. He and Michael Crichton discussed how to adapt the novel to a film. Crichton asked Spielberg how he planned to create the dinosaurs. Spielberg shrugged and said, "Not important. Not what we need to talk about. . . . Effects are only as good as the audience's feeling for the characters."[3] The director then talked about each character in the story and how he wanted them portrayed in the film. Crichton wrote a screenplay, and then Spielberg brought in other writers to streamline and focus the script.

Although Spielberg knew that the script was a vital ingredient in making the film, he also knew that in a movie about dinosaurs, the dinosaurs had to look realistic. He hired a team of artists, sculptors, engineers, and skilled craftsmen to create believable looking dinosaurs.

The dinosaurs were a combination of life-sized robots and computer animation. Stan Winston and the other special effects artists spent one year working with paleontologists to make sure the dinosaurs in the film were true to what experts think dinosaurs really looked like. They also studied large animals, including elephants, giraffes, and whales to see how their muscles moved.

The Tyrannosaurus rex they built was twenty feet tall, weighed thirteen thousand pounds, and was made from a frame of fiberglass and three thousand pounds of clay, covered with latex skin. It was the largest animatronics (remote controlled) robot ever created for a film. Winston's team of sixty craftsmen also created a velociraptor, brachiosaurus, triceratops, gallimimus, and dilophosaurus for the film.

The rest of the dinosaurs in *Jurassic Park* were computer-generated images created at George Lucas's Industrial Light & Magic studio. Each dinosaur bone had to be drawn, each movement separately rendered. It took fifty computer experts more than eighteen months to create the six and a half minutes of digital dinosaurs used in the film. "Creating computer generated creatures that had been dead for 150 million years wasn't so much a question of capability as it was a matter of sweat. It just took an enormous amount of work," said computer animator Steve Williams.[4]

Filming began in August 1992 on the island of Kauai, Hawaii. On September 11, the last day of the location shoot, Hurricane Iniki struck with a vengeance and flattened the sets. The cast and crew rode out the storm in a hotel ballroom. According to Spielberg, the experience brought them together as "one big terrified family."[5] As soon as they were able to get a flight out of Hawaii, Spielberg and his cast and crew left the island and flew to Hollywood to complete the filming on the Universal and Warner Brothers lots.

Since many of the dinosaurs in *Jurassic Park* were special effects that would be added later, the actors had to pretend the animals were there during filming. They had to act startled or afraid of dinosaurs they could not

Paleontologist Alan Grant (Sam Neill) comes face to face with a terrifying T. rex in 1993's *Jurassic Park*.

see. When a dinosaur was supposed to appear, Spielberg added sound effects to help the actors imagine the scene. According to Laura Dern, who starred in the film, "I'd be in a specific moment and something's about to appear and I'm supposed to feel the utmost terror a human being can ever feel in their life and I'd hear, 'Rrrrrroarrrrrr! Rrrrrrroarrrrrr!' in the background."[6] She often felt more amused than terrified.

Filming on *Jurassic Park* was completed in Hollywood on November 30, 1992, twelve days ahead of schedule and on budget. Special effects, sound effects, and music needed to be added to the film before it would be ready for theaters. While the various teams worked to finish *Jurassic Park*, Spielberg turned to his next project, the film version of Thomas Keneally's novel, *Schindler's List*.

Spielberg read *Schindler's List* when it was released in 1982. He was immediately drawn to the story, and Universal Studios purchased the film rights for him. *Schindler's List* is the story of a German businessman named Oskar Schindler who saved more than one thousand Jews from being killed by the Nazis during World War II. The book paints a graphic picture of the Holocaust, the slaughter of more than six million people.

Spielberg thought about making *Schindler's List* for years but kept putting it off. It was a much weightier subject than he had ever attempted to film and far from the typical "feel good" entertainment he usually made. Many people in the film industry felt that Spielberg was not serious enough to make *Schindler's List*. Spielberg worried about that, too. "It has to

The Great Murders

Spielberg grew up listening to stories about family friends and relatives who died in the Holocaust. But his parents did not call it the Holocaust. They called it "the Great Murders."[7] His grandmother gave English lessons to Holocaust survivors. As a child, Spielberg learned his numbers from one of her students. The numbers had been burned into the man's arm at the Auschwitz concentration camp in southern Poland. The tattoo was used to identify him as a prisoner of the camp. "He taught me what a two was and a four and a seven," said Spielberg, "and he did a little magic trick when he showed me a nine—he flipped his forearm and said it was a six."[8]

be accurate," he said, "and it has to be fair and it cannot *in the least* come across as entertainment. And it's very hard when you're making a movie, not to violate one or all of those self-imposed rules."[9]

One of the reasons he finally committed to the project was that his attitude about being Jewish had changed. As a child, he had been ashamed to admit he was a Jew. Then, for years he ignored his faith. After he married Kate Capshaw, Spielberg and his wife realized they wanted to raise their children in a Jewish home. Spielberg taught his children about Jewish holidays and traditions and practiced his faith with his family. "I was feeling proud to be a Jew and I was feeling fulfilled by being able to state this without fear of not belonging," he said.[10]

To prepare for *Schindler's List*, Spielberg studied the time period, watched documentaries about World War II, and learned all he could about the Holocaust. He visited the Auschwitz concentration camp in southern Poland. Spielberg felt it was important to show how a single person can change the world for good in the midst of unspeakable evil. He also wanted to make sure the Holocaust was not forgotten. "I'm making this film for myself, for the survivors, for my family—and for people who should understand the meaning of the word 'Holocaust,'" he said.[11]

Spielberg began filming *Schindler's List* in and around Krakow, Poland, in March 1993. It was a massive production with 126 speaking parts, 30,000 extras, and 148 sets on 35 locations. The World Jewish Congress would not allow Spielberg to film inside Auschwitz, so Spielberg built a replica camp outside the Auschwitz gate. Filming was also done at Schindler's factory and apartment building. Many scenes were filmed outdoors in temperatures of fifteen below zero. "Nobody complained about how we were suffering from the cold," said cinematographer Janusz Kaminski, "because our suffering was so little compared with what the actual prisoners were subjected to."[12]

Spielberg shot *Schindler's List* with black and white film. Studio executives tried to persuade him to shoot in color so the film would be more marketable. Spielberg refused. He insisted that black and white was needed to bring realism to the film. He often used hand held cameras to give the film the look of a documentary news story. "Nothing about this movie is in my so-called style," he said. "Until now, everything in my life was still through an attractive lens."[13]

Spielberg usually does not allow visitors on the sets of his films. He made an exception on *Schindler's List* and allowed Holocaust survivors to visit the set. They often told Spielberg stories of their experiences and pointed out specific locations for actual events. One survivor told Spielberg how prisoners pricked their fingers and used the blood to color their cheeks to give them a rosy, healthy glow. Spielberg added the incident to the film.

Kate Capshaw, Spielberg's wife, and their five children flew to Poland and stayed in a small hotel during the filming of *Schindler's List.* They provide much needed emotional support for Spielberg during the difficult weeks of filming. "Every day in Poland I was aware that as a Jew I couldn't have been in Europe 50 years ago," said Spielberg.[14]

It was an emotionally draining time for the director. "Jewish life came pouring back into my heart," he said. "I cried all the time."[15] Spielberg called his friend Robin Williams twice during production and said, "I haven't laughed in seven weeks. Help me here."[16] Williams cheered up his friend by doing comedy routines over the telephone.

While Spielberg filmed *Schindler's List,* he supervised the special effects and music for *Jurassic Park.* During the day he worked on *Schindler,* nights and weekends, he edited *Jurassic.* Since he was in Poland and the staff working on *Jurassic Park* was in Los Angeles, Spielberg rented two satellite channels through a Warsaw, Poland, television station and downloaded the special effects, sound effects, and musical score from the United States.

Jurassic Park was released in June 1993 and quickly broke *E.T.*'s record to become the highest-grossing film of all time up to that point. The critics loved it.

Steven Spielberg on the cover of *Time*, May 19, 1997.

Richard Corliss wrote in *Time* magazine, "It was the director who put the drama in every snazzy frame. For dinosaurs to rule the earth again, the monsters needed majesty as well as menace. And Spielberg got it all right."[17] More than one thousand officially licensed products, such as action figures, lunch boxes, and clothing, were linked to the film and one billion dollars worth of merchandise was sold.

Schindler's List was released in December 1993. People around the world called it "a masterpiece," "inspired," "the greatest film about the Holocaust ever made." James Verniere's review in the *Boston Herald* was typical. "*Schindler's List* is Spielberg's long-awaited dramatic triumph," he wrote. "It is not only a major addition to the body of work about the Holocaust, it is also an undeniably great movie."[18]

There were a handful of critics who objected to the fact that Spielberg focused *Schindler's List* on one thousand Jews who lived instead of the six million who died. The film looked squarely at the horror of the Holocaust yet, in typical Spielberg fashion, ended on a hopeful note. But hope is the common thread that runs thorough all of Steven Spielberg's films. He is the most successful director in history because his films encourage us to believe that good will triumph over evil and an ordinary person can make a difference in the world.

Spielberg did not think *Schindler's List* would be a

financially successful movie. After all, it was a three hour black-and-white film about one of the darkest events in human history. It was also starkly realistic. The scenes of random violence and cruel slaughter were difficult to watch. To Spielberg's surprise, *Schindler's List* became a box-office success. The film earned more than 320 million dollars worldwide. *Schindler's List* also won seven Academy Awards, including two for Steven Spielberg: Best Director and Best Picture.

The year 1993 ended for Steven Spielberg with the most commercially successful film of his career, *Jurassic Park*, and the most critically acclaimed film of his career, *Schindler's List*. Exhausted from the strain of tackling two such difficult projects in one year, Spielberg took some much needed time off from directing. "I have no idea what to do next," he said. "And, more important, I don't care."[19]

9

THE MATURE SPIELBERG

After *Schindler's List* was released in 1993, Steven Spielberg did not direct a film for nearly three years. But they were three of the busiest years of his life. He spent lots of time at home with his wife, Kate Capshaw, and their growing family. "It takes good running shoes to keep up with Kate," said Spielberg. "She has an agenda of things to do, and every morning she wakes everybody up with an explosion of energy and leads us through the day."[1]

Spielberg's primary home was a Mediterranean-style mansion in the Pacific Palisades, a suburb of Los Angeles. The family spent most of their time in the kitchen. On one wall hung a large board that kept track of everyone's activities. Karate lessons and art classes appeared next to Spielberg's schedule. "There's also this couch," said

Capshaw, "which is Steven Central. He has a bunch of scripts to read, and tapes—casting reels, dailies, bits of animation—that he pops into the VCR. But if one of the kids asks him to build a castle, he's immediately down on the floor, building that castle."[2] At night Spielberg, the master storyteller, told stories to his children. "In those three years I probably told more stories at my kids' bedtime than I did to the public in my entire career," he said.[3]

When Kate Capshaw married Steven Spielberg, she took a break from acting to care for their family. In 1994, she returned to acting. She starred in four films in a row. Spielberg had mixed feelings about her work. He preferred her to stay at home. "I'm selfish about my wife," he said. "I want her all to myself."[4]

During his time away from a movie set, Spielberg often thought about the Holocaust survivors he had met in Poland during the filming of *Schindler's List*. Many of them had shared their stories of survival with him. They had described what had happened to them during the war and how they had survived. Spielberg was inspired by their testimonies. He wanted to tell their stories to the world. "It is essential that we see the faces of the survivors, hear their voices and understand," he said. "Only in this way can we ensure that the next generation will not tolerate what the last ignored."[5]

The Spielberg Family

The Spielbergs have seven children: Jessica Capshaw, Max, Theo, Mikaela, Sasha, Sawyer, and Destry.

In 1994, Spielberg used his profits from *Schindler's List* to create the Survivors of the Shoah Visual History Foundation (*Shoah* is the Hebrew word for "Holocaust"). Survivors told volunteers about their lives before, during, and after World War II. Their stories were recorded on film. Between 1994 and 1999, volunteers traveled around the world and interviewed over fifty-two thousand survivors from fifty-six countries in thirty-two languages. The Shoah foundation testimonies are the world's largest visual history archive with more than one hundred twenty thousand hours of testimonies about the Holocaust.

The testimonies were then indexed and catalogued. Schools and libraries can access the testimonies through the Internet. If someone wants to hear a specific story, they can enter a key word and search, much like you search a text document for a word or a phrase. Spielberg hopes the testimonies will help eliminate prejudice and bigotry and teach us that we have a responsibility to make the world a more tolerant place.

Spielberg also used part of his profits from *Schindler's List* to establish the Righteous Persons Foundation. The foundation

The Shoah Foundation

In January 2006, the Shoah Foundation partnered with the University of Southern California and was renamed the USC Shoah Foundation Institute for Visual History and Education. It is now permanently housed in the university's College of Letters, Arts and Sciences.

In 2004, *Schindler's List* was released on DVD. Spielberg stands with five Holocaust survivors at the press briefing, which also announced the tenth anniversary of the Shoah Foundation.

funds projects to strengthen Jewish life in the United States and around the world. For example, Operation Understanding is a leadership program for African-American and Jewish teens. The teens learn about each other's history and culture. They participate in a variety of activities designed to promote understanding and wipe out all forms of discrimination. Spielberg said of the Shoah Foundation and the Righteous Persons Foundation, "Among all the things I've done professionally, these are the two things I'm most proud of."[6]

As his personal fortune grew, Spielberg began to

give away his money to help others. Most of his donations went to Holocaust studies and the support of Jewish culture and education. He is also chairman of the Starlight Starbright Foundation, an organization that helps seriously ill children. The Starbright Foundation builds playrooms and teen lounges in hospitals. It provides PCs, educational software, and Internet access to allow patients to stay connected with the world and keep up with their schoolwork. The foundation also provides hospitals with Fun Centers, mobile entertainment units containing a flat-screen television, DVD player, and Nintendo GameCube system.

Although most of Spielberg's gifts are anonymous, others are well known. He had a pediatric hospital wing built at Cedars-Sinai Medical Center in West Hollywood. He funded a scoring stage on the University of Southern California campus. This large recording studio allows conductors to watch a film while conducting an orchestra. The music is recorded and lines up perfectly with the film. Spielberg has also made donations to the School of American Ballet and The Planetary Society.

His break from directing did not stop Spielberg from producing several successful films in the 1990s, including *The Flinstones*, *Casper*, and *Twister*. In May 1994, he opened a restaurant in Los Angeles with Jeffrey Katzenberg called Dive!. The restaurant looked like a giant yellow submarine and sold submarine sandwiches. Every half hour, the restaurant darkened, sirens blared, and red lights flashed. Huge video screens filled with bubbles and the command "Dive!" echoed throughout the room. The effect made it feel like the diners were actually inside a diving submarine. Dive! is no longer open for business. It closed its doors in January 1999.

In October 1994, Steven Spielberg, Jeffrey Katzenberg, and David Geffen joined forces to create a new movie studio. They called themselves the Dream Team and named the studio DreamWorks SKG. "I dream for a living. And Jeffrey works for a living," Spielberg explained. "So kind of like DreamWorks."[7]

DreamWorks planned to make movies, television shows, records, toys, and computer software. Spielberg was in charge of the movie division, but he was still allowed to make films for other studios. He also helped create toys that he hoped would "drive parents crazy."[8] DreamWorks partnered with Microsoft's Bill Gates to develop multimedia products and computer software.

In March 1995, the American Film Institute awarded Spielberg the Lifetime Achievement Award.

DreamWorks SKG

The SKG in DreamWorks SKG stands for each partner's name: S, for Spielberg, director and founder of Amblin Entertainment; K, for Jeffrey Katzenberg, former head of The Walt Disney Company's film studios; and G, for David Geffen, founder of Geffen Records.

Jeffrey Katzenberg, Steven Spielberg, and David Geffen (left to right) formed a new movie studio, DreamWorks SKG, in October 1994.

The award is given to "an individual who, in a fundamental way, advanced the art of film."[9] Over one thousand friends, relatives, and Hollywood personalities attended the black tie dinner. They munched on tiny chocolate baseball caps frosted with an image of E.T. and listened to actors, producers, and directors pay their respects to Spielberg. When Sid Sheinberg gave Spielberg the award, he said, "Although the mysteries and joys of the future are yet to be revealed, he has already given us many of the greatest moments ever put on film."[10]

Spielberg went to one meeting after another in the early days of DreamWorks. One day he looked at his schedule and saw that "every meeting I had scheduled had nothing to do with directing movies."[11] He realized he missed directing and wanted to get behind a camera again. He did so with gusto and directed three vastly different films in one year.

After *Schindler's List,* many people in the entertainment industry wondered if Spielberg would continue to make movies about serious subjects or go back to making adventure films. One interviewer asked Spielberg if he could go back to making sunny, optimistic movies. "Sure I can," said Spielberg, "because I have a sunny, optimistic nature."[12]

Spielberg chose *The Lost World,* the sequel to *Jurassic Park,* for his next film. "I didn't want to do a serious movie after *Schindler's List,*" he said. "Coming back from those three years of not directing, I didn't want to jump into the deep end of the pool, I wanted to step into the shallow end and get used to the water. I wanted to do something familiar."[13] Spielberg planned to direct a variety of films and go back and forth from pure entertainment to socially conscious movies.

Spielberg began filming *The Lost World* for Universal Studios in September 1996. The technology for creating robotic and computer-generated dinosaurs had improved since Spielberg had filmed *Jurassic Park,* so *The Lost World* had more dinosaurs in it than the first film. Spielberg's special effects team created forty-four dinosaur robots. Each robot weighed nearly ten tons and cost as much as one million dollars apiece. "The animals are more involved in helping to tell the story," said Spielberg. "They also have more people to eat because in *The Lost World* there are more characters—many of whom are eminently deserving of being eaten."[14]

Spielberg finished filming *The Lost World*, one of his "entertainment" films, in December 1996. In February 1997, he began filming *Amistad*, one of his "serious" films.

Amistad is based on the true story of an 1839 mutiny aboard a slave ship. It was the first film Spielberg directed for DreamWorks. Spielberg said he chose the story because of his two African-American children, Theo and Mikaela. "I felt very strongly that this is a story they should know about," he said. "And my other children should know about it, too."[15]

Spielberg took great care to make *Amistad* historically accurate. He hired many of its actors from West Africa and had them coached in Mende, the language of the *Amistad* captives. He bound them in real slave chains. Spielberg filmed the torturous journey aboard the slave ship so realistically that many cast and crew members were reduced to tears. "This film will never leave any of us," he said. "We can walk away from the production, but the subject will always be with us."[16]

The Lost World opened in May 1997. It was a box

Matthew McConaughey (leaning against the railing at the bottom right) and Morgan Freeman (in the upper left wearing the top hat) portray abolitionists, people who wanted to end slavery, in the 1997 film *Amistad*.

office hit but most film critics did not care for it. *Amistad* was released in December 1997. The film received mediocre reviews and did not do well at the box office. Most people felt the film was too preachy, more a history lesson than entertainment. Spielberg was disappointed that more people did not go see *Amistad,* but he was proud of the film. "It's just something I'm really glad I had a part in," he said. "This is a story that people of all nationalities and races should know."[17]

Spielberg pleased both moviegoers *and* film critics with his next film.

10

A LASTING LEGACY

Steven Spielberg has always been fascinated with the 1930s, the 1940s, and World War II. He has watched reel after reel of news footage and many documentary films about the war. Although he had looked at various aspects of World War II in his films, Spielberg had never examined combat. He decided to tackle that difficult subject in *Saving Private Ryan*. "I made *Saving Private Ryan* for my father," said Spielberg. "He's the one who filled my head with war stories when I was growing up."[1]

Spielberg was drawn to the film because it was based on a true story. *Saving Private Ryan* tells the story of a squad of eight American soldiers who go on a dangerous mission to find Private James Ryan, a soldier whose three brothers have been killed in combat. As they search for

Ryan, the soldiers question why they should risk their lives to save one soldier.

Spielberg set out to make *Saving Private Ryan* as realistic looking as possible. He hired Vietnam veteran Captain Dale Dye to conduct a military boot camp for the actors. Captain Dye taught the actors how to be soldiers. For ten days, Tom Hanks and his fellow actors crawled in the mud and slept in the dirt. They ate rations, lived in pup tents, marched, and did weapons training. They often worked in the pouring rain. They were cold, and they slept very little. When some of the actors threatened to quit, Tom Hanks, the star of the film, convinced them to finish boot camp.

Spielberg made sure the sets and costumes used in the film were as believable as the actors. His team of designers dug a river and built an entire village in Hatfield, England, just north of London. Then they destroyed parts of it to make it look bombed. They purchased truckloads of rubble from construction sites and spread it over the set. Spielberg hired Porsche engineers to build the German Tiger Tanks used in the film. He hired thousands of soldiers from the Irish army as extras. The costume designer and her team made more than three thousand five hundred uniforms for the film. Each uniform was aged to look worn.

Filming began in June 1997. The opening scene, which lasted twenty-five minutes, took almost a month to shoot. Spielberg wanted the landing on Omaha

Beach to look so realistic that the audience would think the filmmakers were actually on the beach on D-Day. Spielberg used hand-held cameras to give the images an unsteady look. He put the film through a special chemical process to remove some of the color and make it look like film of the 1940s. "I wanted to achieve reality," he said.[2]

Spielberg's goal was to accurately show combat. He did not glamorize the gushing blood and gore. He wanted the film to honor the memory of the men and women who fought. "This movie is for the veterans of World War II," he said. "If

Barry Pepper, Adam Goldberg, Edward Burns, and Tom Sizemore (left to right) play World War II soldiers who risk their lives to rescue one of their own in *Saving Private Ryan.*

it weren't for those veterans, none of us would be having the lives we're having today."[3]

While Spielberg was in Ireland filming *Saving Private Ryan*, he learned about the negative aspects of fame. On July 11, 1997, Los Angeles police arrested Jonathan Norman outside Spielberg's California home. Police found handcuffs, duct tape, razor blades, and a notebook stuffed with photos of Spielberg and his family in Norman's van. Norman was obsessed with Spielberg and had been stalking, or following him, for a long time. He planned to break into the director's home and try to hurt him. When Spielberg heard about the arrest, he "became completely panicked and upset."[4]

Spielberg increased security around his home and testified at Norman's trial. Norman was found guilty of stalking. He had two prior convictions, so under California's three-strikes law, the judge sentenced him to the maximum sentence allowed, twenty-five years to life in prison.

Saving Private Ryan opened in theaters in July 1998. Spielberg did not think the film would be financially successful because the scenes of battle and bloodshed were brutally realistic and difficult to watch. He told Tom Hanks, "Despite you being in this movie, nobody's showing up for this picture."[5] But the film was important to Spielberg and he fretted about the possibility of empty theaters. He wanted huge audiences to see his memorial to the soldiers who fought in World War II. "Whenever I have a movie coming out, I am the same nervous blob of misshapen Jell-O I was when I first began showing those little 8-millimeter films to teeny audiences," he said. "That hasn't changed, and it's a very good thing, because I think all of us do our best work when we're the most frightened."[6]

Spielberg had no reason to worry. *Saving Private Ryan* became a box office hit, the most financially successful war movie ever made. Critics called the film a masterpiece, and World War II veterans praised it for its accurate depiction of war. The film won five Academy Awards, including one for Spielberg for Best Director. "Am I allowed to say I really wanted this?" he said in his acceptance speech. "This is fantastic."[7]

Spielberg has received many awards as a filmmaker. *Entertainment Weekly* named him one of the one hundred greatest entertainers from 1950 through 1999. The American Film Institute included five of Spielberg's films, *Schindler's List, E.T.: The Extra-Terrestrial, Jaws, Raiders of the Lost Ark,* and *Close Encounters of the Third Kind,* on their list of the greatest one hundred films of all time. In January 2000, The Broadcast Film Critics Association named Spielberg the filmmaker of the decade. In March of that year, the Directors Guild of America gave him their Lifetime Achievement Award.

A Degree . . . Finally!

In 2002, Steven Spielberg completed his college degree by taking extension courses from California State University at Long Beach. He received a bachelor's degree in film and electronic arts. He said he went back to get his degree because he wanted to please his father and because he wanted to stress the importance of education to his children. When Spielberg walked across the stage in his cap and gown to accept his diploma, the orchestra played the *Indiana Jones* theme song.

The British Academy of Film and Television Arts awarded Spielberg the Stanley Kubrick Britannia Award for Excellence in Film, and on January 29, 2001, he was awarded an honorary knighthood for his contribution to international film. "Mr. Spielberg's career has had a global impact," said British ambassador Sir Christopher Meyer, when he presented the award.[8]

After *Saving Private Ryan*, Spielberg took a three-year break from directing. In 2001, he wrote the screenplay for and directed *A.I.: Artificial Intelligence*, a science fiction film about a robot boy who wants to be human. The film received mixed reviews. Some critics loved it; others thought it was confusing. But the majority of people found the film thought provoking and intellectually stimulating. *A.I.* did not earn back its production costs when it was released in the United States, but after its worldwide release, it earned over 100 million dollars in profits.

In 2002, Spielberg directed two of his best friends, Tom Cruise, in *Minority Report*, and Tom Hanks, in *Catch Me If You Can*. They were two very different films, one grim and downbeat, the other breezy and light. *Minority Report* is a science fiction story set in the year 2054. Cruise plays the chief of a Washington, D.C., special police unit that relies on psychics to predict crimes. Cruise and his fellow police officers then arrest the criminals before they commit the crimes. *Catch Me If You Can* is based on the true story of Frank Abagnale, Jr.

In 2003, Steven Spielberg received a star on the Hollywood Walk of Fame in Los Angeles, California.

Leonardo DiCaprio plays the part of Abagnale, a sixteen-year-old con artist who successfully impersonated an airline pilot, a doctor, and a lawyer.

Cruise and Hanks both worked with Spielberg a few years later. In 2004, Spielberg directed Tom Hanks in *The Terminal*, and in 2005, he directed Tom Cruise in *War of the Worlds*. A remake of the classic science fiction story by H. G. Wells, *War of the Worlds* was a departure for Spielberg. In his previous films about aliens from outer space, the aliens were friendly. In *War of the Worlds*, they are determined to destroy the earth. With two of the biggest names in Hollywood, Spielberg and Cruise, working together on the film, *War of the Worlds* quickly became a huge box office hit.

Spielberg directed *Munich* in 2005. The film was nominated for five Academy Awards, including two for Spielberg, Best Director and Best Picture. The film did not receive any awards and was a box office disappointment. In December 2005, Spielberg and his partners sold DreamWorks SKG to Viacom, the parent company of Paramount Pictures. The sale was completed in February 2006.

In May 2007, Spielberg returned to television as the creator/executive producer for the FOX television reality show, *On the Lot*. Contestants made short films that were critiqued by judges and voted on by the

public. Spielberg viewed the show as a way to give young filmmakers a start in the business.

Steven Spielberg speaks with actors Tom Cruise and Dakota Fanning on the set of *War of the Worlds* (2004).

In 2007, Spielberg filmed the fourth *Indiana Jones* movie, *Indiana Jones and the Kingdom of the Crystal Skull.* The film stars Harrison Ford, Karen Allen, Shia LaBeouf, and Cate Blanchett, and is scheduled for release in May 2008. Spielberg is also working on a film about Abraham Lincoln. Liam Neeson, the star of *Schindler's List,* has agreed to play the part of Lincoln. Spielberg says he would like to direct a love story, and he vows to direct a musical "even if people laugh it off the face of the earth."[9]

Spielberg never gets tired of telling stories. He

wants to "tell as many great stories to as many people as will listen."[10] He has an endless supply of ideas. "I don't have enough time in a lifetime to tell all the stories I want to tell," he said.[11] Spielberg's longtime friend Tom Hanks agrees. "For every idea Steven makes into a movie, there are a thousand more in his head," said Hanks. "His cranium houses the world's largest multiplex theater—open 24 hours a day."[12]

Many people consider Spielberg the greatest director of the century. "When the history of cinema is written over these decades, Steven Spielberg will be heralded as an innovative, exciting, blistering talent," said Academy Award winning director Richard Attenborough, who played John Hammond in *Jurassic Park*.[13] DreamWorks partner Jeffrey Katzenberg agrees. "He is *the* storyteller of our time," he said of Spielberg. "I don't think there is anyone who has reached as many people with their stories as he has."[14]

Spielberg has often said that the secret to his success as a director was "wanting it more than anything else."[15] He encourages people who want a career in filmmaking to start as young as possible and "do a lot of writing, try to make a short film or two, cut it yourself, also do the photography, and if you're a ham, star in it."[16]

Steven Spielberg has amassed a huge personal fortune and a business empire. "I've never been in it for the money," he said. "I was in it for the physical pleasure of filmmaking. It's a physical pleasure being on a set, making a movie, you know—taking images out of your imagination and making them three-dimensional and solid. It's magic."[17] Spielberg's passion for movies shows in his films. "I love telling stories," he said. "When I get tired of telling stories publicly I'll retire and I'll tell stories to my kids. But I don't think that'll ever happen. I love doing this job. It's a great job!"[18]

CHRONOLOGY

1946   Steven Spielberg is born on December 18 in Cincinnati, Ohio.

1949   The Spielbergs move to Haddonfield, New Jersey.

1957   The Spielbergs move to Phoenix, Arizona.

1964   On March 24, Steven shows his first feature-length film, *Firelight*, in a Phoenix, Arizona, movie theater. Moves to Saratoga, California.

1965   Graduates from Saratoga High School. His parents divorce. Attends California State University at Long Beach.

1968   Directs *Amblin'* and signs a contract with Universal Studios to direct television shows.

1971   Directs *Duel,* a television movie.

1972   Expanded theatrical version of *Duel* released in theaters.

1974   *The Sugarland Express* released in theaters.

1975   *Jaws* opens in theaters and becomes the most successful film in history up to that time.

1977   *Close Encounters of the Third Kind* opens to critical and commercial acclaim.

1981   *Raiders of the Lost Ark* released.

1982   *E.T.: The Extra-Terrestrial* and *Poltergeist* released. Forms Amblin Entertainment.

1985   Marries Amy Irving. Son Max Samuel born. *The Color Purple* released. Created television show *Amazing Stories*.

1987   Receives the Irving G. Thalberg Memorial Award from the Academy of Motion Picture Arts and Sciences for his special contributions to the film industry.

1989   Spielberg and Amy Irving divorce.

1990   Daughter Sasha born.

1991   Steven Spielberg marries Kate Capshaw. Son Theo adopted. *Hook* released in theaters.

1992   Son Sawyer born.

1993   *Jurassic Park* and *Schindler's List* released.

1994   Wins Best Director and Best Picture Academy awards for *Schindler's List*. Creates the Survivors of the Shoah Visual History Foundation and the Righteous Persons Foundation. Starts his own movie studio, DreamWorks SKG.

1995   Receives the Lifetime Achievement Award from the American Film Institute.

1996   Adopts daughter Mikeala. Daughter Destry born.

1998   *Saving Private Ryan* released.

1999 Spielberg wins Best Director Academy award for *Saving Private Ryan.*

2000 The Broadcast Film Critics Association names Steven Spielberg the filmmaker of the decade. Receives the Directors Guild of America Lifetime Achievement Award.

2001 His Royal Highness Prince Andrew of England awards Spielberg the Stanley Kubrick Britannia Award for Excellence in Film. Spielberg is awarded an honorary knighthood in a ceremony at the British Embassy in Washington. *A.I.: Artificial Intelligence* released.

2002 Receives a bachelor's degree in film and electronic arts from California State University at Long Beach. *Minority Report* and *Catch Me If You Can* released.

2004 *The Terminal* released.

2005 *War of the Worlds* and *Munich* released. Sells DreamWorks SKG.

FILMOLOGY

Motion Pictures Directed by Steven Spielberg

Duel (1971)

The Sugarland Express (1974)

Jaws (1975)

Close Encounters of the Third Kind (1977)

1941 (1979)

Raiders of the Lost Ark (1981)

E.T.: The Extra-Terrestrial (1982)

Twilight Zone—The Movie, "Kick the Can" (1983)

Indiana Jones and the Temple of Doom (1984)

The Color Purple (1985)

Empire of the Sun (1987)

Indiana Jones and the Last Crusade (1989)

Always (1989)

Hook (1991)

Jurassic Park (1993)

Schindler's List (1993)

The Lost World (1997)

Amistad (1997)

Saving Private Ryan (1998)

A.I.: Artificial Intelligence (2001)

Minority Report (2002)

Catch Me If You Can (2002)

The Terminal (2004)

War of the Worlds (2005)

Munich (2005)

Indiana Jones and the Kingdom of the Crystal Skull (2008)

CHAPTER NOTES

Chapter 1. One More Scream

1. "Summer of the Shark," (cover story), *Time*, June 23, 1975, p. 44.

2. Joseph McBride, *Steven Spielberg: A Biography* (New York: Da Capo Press, 1999), p. 246.

3. Steven Spielberg, *JAWS: 30th Anniversary Edition Commemorative Photo Journal* (Universal Studios, 2005), p. 31.

4. Philip Taylor, *Steven Spielberg: The Man, His Movies and Their Meaning* (New York: Continuum, 1999), p. 87.

5. Laurent Bouzereau, *Spotlight on Location: The Making of Jaws* (Universal Studios Home Video, 2000).

6. Robert J. Emery, *The Directors: The Films of Steven Spielberg* (Media Entertainment, Inc., 1999).

7. Stephen Schiff, "Seriously Spielberg," *The New Yorker*, March 21, 1994, p. 107.

8. Tony Crawley, *The Steven Spielberg Story* (New York: Quill, 1983), p. 44.

9. Laurent Bouzereau, *30th Anniversary Edition: The Making of Jaws* (MCA Home Video, Inc., Universal Studios Home Video, 2005).

10. Julie Chen, "Spielberg Proudest of Schindler's List: New Kennedy Center Honoree Reviews Career Highlights with Julie Chen," *CBS News: The Early Show Celeb Spot*, December 26, 2006, <http://www.cbsnews.com/stories/2006/12/26/earlyshow/leisure/celebspot/printable2297610.shtml> (May 1, 2007).

Chapter 2. Creative Naughtiness

1. Douglas Brode, *The Films of Steven Spielberg* (New York: Citadel Press, 2000), p. 14.

2. John Skow, "Staying Five Moves Ahead," *Time*, May 31, 1982, p. 58.

3. Richard Corliss, "Steve's Summer Magic," *Time*, May 31, 1982, p. 57.

4. Denise Worrell, "The Autobiography of Peter Pan," *Time*, July 15, 1985, p. 62.

5. Ibid., p. 63.

6. Joseph McBride, *Steven Spielberg: A Biography* (New York: Da Capo Press, 1999), p. 72.

7. Julie Salamon, "The Long Voyage Home," *Harper's Bazaar*, February 1994, p. 136.

8. David Breskin, "The *Rolling Stone* Interview: Steven Spielberg," *Rolling Stone*, October 24, 1985, p. 74.

9. Lynn Hirschberg, "Will Hollywood's Mr. Perfect Ever Grow Up?" *Rolling Stone*, July 19–August 2, 1984, p. 35.

10. Steve Poster, "The Mind Behind *Close Encounters of the Third Kind*," *Steven Spielberg Interviews* (Jackson, Miss.: University Press of Mississippi, 2000), p. 56.

11. Richard Corliss, "I Dream for a Living," *Time*, July 15, 1985, p. 56.

12. McBride, p. 12.

13. Worrell, p. 63.

14. McBride, p. 101.

15. Laurent Bouzereau, *The Making of Close Encounters of the Third Kind* (Columbia Tristar Home Video, Inc., 1997).

Chapter 3. Learning the Biz at Universal Studios

1. Joseph McBride, *Steven Spielberg: A Biography* (New York: Da Capo Press, 1999), p. 113.

2. Ibid., p. 110.

3. Julie Salamon, "The Long Voyage Home," *Harper's Bazaar*, February 1994, p. 186.

4. Ibid.

5. Denise Worrell, "The Autobiography of Peter Pan," *Time*, July 15, 1985, p. 63.

6. Gene Siskel, "Spielberg Tells Why He's Films' Most Successful Director," *Chicago Tribune*, June 6, 1982.

7. Richard Corliss, "I Dream for a Living," *Time*, July 15, 1985, p. 57.

8. McBride, p. 162.

9. Lynn Hirschberg, "Will Hollywood's Mr. Perfect Ever Grow Up?" *Rolling Stone*, July 19–August 2, 1984, p. 35.

10. McBride, p. 166.

11. Hirschberg, p. 35.

12. Ibid.

13. Richard Corliss, "Steve's Summer Magic," *Time*, May 31, 1982, p. 57.

Chapter 4. I Want a Hit!

1. Judith Crist, *Take 22: Moviemakers on Moviemaking* (New York: Viking, 1984), p. 358.

2. Philip Taylor, *Steven Spielberg: The Man, His Movies and Their Meaning* (New York: Continuum, 1999), p. 79.

3. Stephen King, *Danse Macabre* (New York: Everest House Publishers, 1981), p. 163.

4. Robert J. Emery, *The Directors: The Films of Steven Spielberg* (Media Entertainment, Inc., 1999).

5. Judy Klemesrud, "Can He Make the 'Jaws' of Outer Space?" *New York Times*, May 15, 1977.

6. Ibid.

7. Robert J. Emery, *The Directors: The Films of Steven Spielberg* (Media Entertainment, Inc., 1999).

8. Klemesrud.

9. Lee Grant, "Spielberg's 'Close Encounters,'" Los Angeles Times, March 14, 1977.

10. Frank Rich, "The Aliens Are Coming!" *Time*, November 7, 1977, p. 103.

Chapter 5. Blockbusters

1. Stephen Rowley, "Steven Spielberg," *Senses of Cinema*, January 2006, <http://www.sensesofcinema.com/contents/directors/06/spielberg.html> (April 10, 2007).

2. Bill Davidson, "Will '1941' Make Spielberg a Billion-Dollar Baby?" *New York Times*, December 9, 1979.

3. "Dialogue on Film: Steven Spielberg," *American Film*, June 1988, p. 15.

4. Andrew C. Bobrow, "Filming *The Sugarland Express*: An Interview with Steven Spielberg," *Steven Spielberg Interviews* (Jackson, Miss.: University Press of Mississippi, 2000), p. 27.

5. Laurent Bouzereau, *Indiana Jones, Making the Trilogy: Raiders of the Lost Ark* (Lucasfilm, Ltd., 2003).

6. Ibid.

7. Janet Maslin, "How Old Movie Serials Inspired Lucas and Spielberg," *New York Times*, June 7, 1981.

8. John Baxter, *Steven Spielberg: The Unauthorized Biography* (New York: HarperCollins, 1997), p. 214.

9. Robert J. Emery, *The Directors: The Films of Steven Spielberg* (Media Entertainment, Inc., 1999).

10. Michiko Kakutani, "The Two Faces of Spielberg: Horror vs. Hope," *New York Times*, May 30, 1982.

11. Linda Sunshine, editor, *E.T. The Extra-Terrestrial: From Concept to Classic* (New York: New Market Press, 2002), p. 8.

12. Tony Crawley, *The Steven Spielberg Story* (New York: Quill, 1983), p. 118.

13. "Creating a Creature," *Time*, May 31, 1982, p. 60.

14. Richard Corliss, "Steve's Summer Magic," *Time*, May 31, 1982, p. 54.

15. Sunshine, p. 8.

16. Emery.

17. Kakutani.

18. Frank Sanello, *Spielberg: The Man, the Movies, the Mythology* (Lanham, Md.: Taylor Trade Publishing, 2002) p. 103.

Chapter 6. A Film Company and a Movie For Grown-ups

1. Richard Corliss, "I Dream for a Living," *Time*, July 15, 1985, p. 56.

2. Ann Bayer and Nancy Griffin, "Spielberg: Husband, Father and Hitmaker," *Life*, May 1986, p. 156.

3. "Terrestrial Sphere: Steven Spielberg's Hollywood Headquarters," *Architectural Digest*, May 1985, p. 197.

4. Jack Kroll, "The Wizard of Wonderland," *Newsweek*, June 4, 1984, p. 83.

5. Laurent Bouzereau, *Indiana Jones, Making the Trilogy: The Temple of Doom* (Lucasfilm, Ltd., 2003).

6. Aljean Harmetz, "Hollywood Plans New Rating To Protect Children Under 13," *New York Times*, June 20, 1984.

7. Ralph Novak, "Picks & Pans, Screen: Indiana Jones and the Temple of Doom," *People*, June 4, 1984, p. 12.

8. Richard Corliss, "I Dream for a Living," *Time*, July 15, 1985, p. 61.

9. Glenn Collins, "New Departures For Two Major Directors," *New York Times*, December 15, 1985.

10. Corliss, p. 61.

11. Bayer and Griffin, p. 149.

12. Andrew Yule, *Steven Spielberg: Father of the Man* (London: Warner Books, 1997), p. 32.

13. Cathleen McGuigan, "Whoopee For Whoopi," *Newsweek*, December 30, 1985, p. 60.

14. "Cosmo Tells All: Couple of the Month," *Cosmopolitan*, September 1984, p. 220.

15. Gene Siskel, "Color Purple: Powerful, Daring, Sweetly Uplifting," *Chicago Tribune*, December 20, 1985.

16. Gerald Early, "*The Color Purple* as Everybody's Protest Art," *The Films of Steven Spielberg: Critical Essays* (Lanham, Maryland: The Scarecrow Press, Inc., 2002), p. 94.

Chapter 7. Family Man

1. "Dialogue on Film: Steven Spielberg," *American Film*, June 1988, p. 12.

2. Myra Forsberg, "Spielberg at 40: The Man and the Child," *New York Times*, January 10, 1988.

3. Ibid.

4. "Irving G. Thalberg Memorial Award," *Academy of Motion Picture Arts and Sciences*, n.d., <www.oscars.org/aboutacademyawards/awards/thalberg.html> (August 3, 2006).

5. Steven Spielberg, "1986 (59th) Academy Awards Irving G. Thalberg Memorial Award: Steven Spielberg," Academy Film Archive, Acceptance Speech, March 31, 1987.

6. Susan Royal, "*Always*: An Interview With Steven Spielberg," *American Premiere*, December 1989/January 1990, p. 8.

7. Forsberg.

8. Joseph McBride, *Steven Spielberg: A Biography* (New York: Da Capo Press, 1999), p. 401.

9. Philip Taylor, *Steven Spielberg: The Man, His Movies and Their Meaning* (New York: Continuum, 1999), p. 112.

10. Laurent Bouzereau, *Indiana Jones, Making the Trilogy: The Last Crusade* (Lucasfilm, Ltd., 2003).

11. Vincent Canby, "Spielberg's Elixir Shows Signs of Mature Magic," *New York Times*, June 18, 1989.

12. Sherry Suib Cohen, "Don't Call Her Mrs. Spielberg," *McCall's*, May 1999, p. 46.

13. Ibid.

14. Richard Corliss and Jeffrey Ressner, "Peter Pan Grows Up But Can He Still Fly?" *Time*, May 19, 1997, p. 82.

15. Denise Worrell, "The Autobiography of Peter Pan," *Time*, July 15, 1985, p. 63.

16. Clifford Terry, "Spielberg in Neverland: Hollywood Bets His Old Magic Will Work Again," *Chicago Tribune*, December 8, 1991.

17. Forsberg.

Chapter 8. Dinosaurs and Death Camps

1. Tom Shone, *Blockbuster: How the Jaws and Jedi Generation Turned Hollywood into a Boom-Town* (New York: Scribner, 2005), p. 216.

2. Stephen Schiff, "Seriously Spielberg," *The New Yorker*, March 21, 1994, p. 101.

3. Joseph McBride, *Steven Spielberg: A Biography* (New York: Simon & Schuster, 1997), p. 421.

4. Don Shay and Jody Duncan, *The Making of Jurassic Park: An Adventure 65 Million Years in the Making* (New York: Ballantine Books, 1993), p. 128.

5. David Wild, "Jurassic Spark," *Rolling Stone*, June 24, 1993, p. 37.

6. Robert J. Emery, *The Directors: The Films of Steven Spielberg* (Media Entertainment, Inc., 1999).

7. Peter Travers, "Steven Spielberg," *Rolling Stone: The Fortieth Anniversary*, May 3–17, 2007, p. 96.

8. Lisa Grunwald, "Steven Spielberg Gets Real," *Life*, December 1993, p. 48.

9. Susan Royal, "*Always*: An Interview with Steven Spielberg," *American Premiere*, December 1989/January 1990, p. 12.

10. Edward Guthmann, "Spielberg's 'List,'" *Oskar Schindler and His List: The Man, the Book, the Film, the Holocaust and Its Survivors* (Forest Dale, Vt.: Paul S. Eriksson, 1995), p. 53.

11. Andrew Nagorski, "Spielberg's Risk," *Newsweek*, May 24, 1993, p. 61.

12. Anne Thompson, "Making History: How Steven Spielberg Brought *Schindler's List* To Life," *Entertainment Weekly*, January 21, 1994, p. 18–19.

13. Grunwald, p. 54.

14. Ibid, p. 50.

15. David Ansen, "Spielberg's Obsession," *Newsweek*, December 20, 1993, p. 115.

16. Ibid.

17. Richard Corliss and David S. Jackson, "*Jaws II*," *Time*, June 14, 1993, p. 70.

18. James Verniere, "Holocaust Drama is a Spielberg Triumph," *The Boston Herald*, December 15, 1993.

19. Schiff, p. 100.

Chapter 9. The Mature Spielberg

1. Melina Gerosa, "Loving Steven," *Ladies' Home Journal*, October 1994, p. 160.

2. Richard Corliss and Jeffrey Ressner, "Peter Pan Grows Up But Can He Still Fly?" *Time*, May 19, 1997, p. 78.

3. Ibid.

4. Gerosa, p. 160.

5. Linden Gross, "Steven Spielberg's Close Encounter With the Past," *Reader's Digest*, April 1996, p. 76.

6. Stephen Dubner, "Steven the Good," *New York Times Magazine*, February 14, 1999, p. 43.

7. Larry King, "Steven Spielberg Discusses His Career in Movies and Television," *Larry King Live* transcript, December 8, 1999, p. 21.

8. Richard Corliss, "Hey, Let's Put On a Show!" *Time*, March 27, 1995, p. 59.

9. George Stevens, Jr., *The American Film Institute 23rd Annual Life Achievement Award: A Salute to Steven Spielberg* (Republic Entertainment, Inc., 1995).

10. Ibid.

11. Richard Corliss and Jeffrey Ressner, "Peter Pan Grows Up But Can He Still Fly?" *Time*, May 19, 1997, p. 78.

12. Frank Sanello, *Spielberg: The Man, the Movies, the Mythology* (Lanham, Md.: Taylor Trade Publishing, 2002), p. 236.

13. Peter Biskind, "A World Apart," *Premiere*, May 1997, p. 73.

14. Jeffrey Ressner, "I Wanted To See a T. Rex Stomping Down a Street," *Time*, May 19, 1997, p. 82.

15. Bruce Newman, "On Location: Spielberg's Children Inspired Him to Recount the Amistad Mutiny of 1839," *Los Angeles Times*, November 9, 1997.

16. Steven Spielberg, "Amistad Production Notes," DreamWorks, SKG, 1997.

17. Ibid.

Chapter 10. A Lasting Legacy

1. J. D. Reed, "Steven Spielberg," *People*, March 15–22, 1999, p. 138.

2. Douglas Brode, *The Films of Steven Spielberg* (New York: Kensington Publishing Corp., 2000), p. 265.

3. Laurent Bouzereau, *The Making of* Saving Private Ryan (DreamWorks SKG, 2004).

4. Cynthia Sanz, "Close Encounter," *People*, February 23, 1998, p. 130.

5. Kenneth Turan, "Steven Spielberg: The Thrill Isn't Gone," *Los Angeles Times*, December 28, 1998.

6. Ibid.

7. Steven Spielberg, "Acceptance Speech at 71st Academy Awards for Best Achievement in Directing for *Saving Private Ryan*," 1998.

8. "Spielberg Receives Royal Honour," *BBC News*, January 30, 2001, <http://news.bbc.co.uk/1/hi/entertainment/1142446.stm> (July 25, 2006).

9. Jess Cagle, "Spielberg's List: What a Director Who Has It All Wants to Do Next," *Time*, June 24, 2002, p. 61.

10. Ronald Grover, "Steven Spielberg: The Storyteller," *Business Week*, July 13, 1998, p. 96.

11. Ibid., p. 102.

12. Elaine Dutka, "On Filmdom's A-List of a Lifetime: Steven Spielberg Receives AFI's Award for Cinematic Achievement," *Los Angeles Times*, March 4, 1995.

13. Don Shay and Jody Duncan, *The Making of* Jurassic Park: *An Adventure 65 Million Years in the Making* (New York: Ballantine Books, 1993), p. 122.

14. Reed, p. 138.

15. Andrew C. Bobrow, "Filming *The Sugarland Express*: An Interview with Steven Spielberg," *Steven Spielberg Interviews* (Jackson, Miss.: University Press of Mississippi, 2000), p. 29.

16. Ibid., p. 28.

17. Stephen Schiff, "Seriously Spielberg," *The New Yorker*, March 21, 1994, pp. 100–101.

18. Robert J. Emery, *The Directors: The Films of Steven Spielberg* (Media Entertainment, Inc., 1999).

FURTHER READING

Hill, Anne E. *Ten American Movie Directors: The Men Behind the Camera.* Berkeley Heights. N.J.: Enslow Publishers, Inc., 2003.

Hillman, Laura. *I Will Plant You a Lilac Tree: A Memoir of a Schindler's List Survivor.* New York: Atheneum Books for Young Readers, 2005.

Kotzwinkle, William. *E.T.: The Book of the Green Planet.* New York: Simon & Schuster, 1985.

Mason, Jane. *Jurassic Park: The Movie Storybook.* New York: Grosset & Dunlap, 1993.

Rubin, Susan Goldman. *Steven Spielberg: Crazy for Movies.* New York: Harry N. Abrams, Inc., 2001.

Schoell, William. *Magic Man: The Life and Films of Steven Spielberg.* Greensboro, N.C.: Tudor Publishers, 1998.

Sirimarco, Elizabeth. *Steven Spielberg: Behind the Camera.* Philadelphia: Chelsea House Publishers, 2002.

INTERNET ADDRESSES

Operation Understanding
http://www.oudc.org

The Shoah Foundation
http://www.vhf.org

The Starlight Starbright Children's Foundation
http://www.starlight.org

Steven Spielberg Films
http://www.spielbergfilms.com

INDEX